Truth and the Comedic Art

Truth and the Comedic Art

Michael Gelven

State University of New York Press

Published by
State University of New York Press

For information, address
State University of New York Press, State University Plaza, Albany, NY 12246

Production by Kelli Williams
Marketing by Michael Campochiaro

Library of Congress Cataloging-in-Publication Data

Gelven, Michael.
Truth and the comedic art / Michael Gelven.
p. cm.
Includes index.
ISBN 0-7914-4663-8 (HC : alk. paper)—ISBN 0-7914-4664-6 (PB : alk. paper)
1. Comedy—History and criticism. 2. European drama (Comedy)—History and criticism. 3. Shakespeare, William, 1564–1616. As you like it. 4. Mozart, Wolfgang Amadeus, 1756–1791. Nozze di Figaro. 5. Wilde, Oscar, 1854–1900. Ideal husband. I. Title.
PN1922.G38 2000
809.2'523—dc21 99-058135

10 9 8 7 6 5 4 3 2 1

Contents

Acknowledgments

Tom Nugent: At the beginning, you challenged me with your preference for tragedy; may this, together with the dramas we shared together, show comedies have greatness, too. Thanks for your friendship, and being my undergraduate apprentice.

Donald Livington: For so many years you served as my mentor to slow erudition. I am grateful for all you've done, both as critic and friend.

Tom Schall and Annette Dixon: My west coast resources for living well. Our too rare visits still sparkle; some of our three-way conversations should go down in history. All three of us need a bit more comedic art in our lives.

Herman Stark: With whom else have I shared so many great comedies, talked about them, and learned from them together? Thank you for reading the manuscript.

Thanks to the Lyric Opera of Chicago and Shakespeare Repertory of Chicago, and all the wonderful store-front theatres on the north and near-north who put on such spirited Shakespeare.

1

Comic Laughter

ONLY the rational can be foolish. To say this is neither sophistry nor cleverness, nor is it an enigma; it is rather the ineluctable and ironic truth. Only those endowed with the faculty of reason are capable of being foolish and recognizing folly, and consequently they alone are enabled to respond to this self-discovery by means of what is perhaps the most curious manifestation of reflective reason, laughter. The captains or custodians of reason, the philosophers, are ironically often the most inept in their attempt to understand its nature. Perhaps no one will ever succeed in capturing its full essence, for its very intimacy makes all articulation of it seem alien; but so many thinkers have struggled with this issue to such a high degree of unsuccess that their efforts induce the very phenomenon they seek to explain. Descartes's definition of laughter is a howler. He describes the purely mechanistic functions of the body without indicating anything that would cause or provoke such a reaction. More profound thinkers, such as Kant, Schopenhauer, Aristotle, Hegel, and even Plato, argue that reason is the origin of mirth. They, however, in various ways, suggest it is somehow our reason being confronted with the irrational that causes the reaction. Thus, Kant, for example, argues that the distinction between the basic faculties of our consciousness, such as the sensibility and the understanding, in what he calls "the free play of the faculties," in a response to surprise, accounts for our mirth. Aristotle, in speaking of comedy, points out that the origin of our amusement is our reaction to the ridiculous. These suggestions are superior to Descartes's because they render an account of *why* we laugh and not merely *how* we laugh, and they wisely spot our ability to reason as crucial. Their accounts are overly narrow, however. We do not always ridicule the hapless comic, nor are we always surprised when we laugh. Indeed, the causes of laughter, as we shall note shortly below, are far too myriad to locate in single phenomenon, and this prolixity of causes confronts us with a methodological paradox.

If there are multiple causes for mirth, and if to make sense of laughter we must do more than merely describe its physiological reactions, then it would seem the present task is too daunting. Even were we able to compile an adequate list, gathered by sheer cataloging of experience, the multiplicity and length of such a list would be entirely unhelpful. Yet, unless we give some account of its cause, we seem to fall back on such vague principles or presuppositions about our consciousness that we are left with purely formal accounts that, being formal, are almost as comically unhelpful as is Cartesian mechanism. It is helpful to realize there may be different ways to be conscious, and that laughter is enabled by their difference or their interaction; but such enlightenment does not provide us with causes or even with phenomenal depictions that are adequate to all cases.

Perhaps, however, the very multiplicity of causes suggests there are different *kinds* of laughter; and perhaps among the kinds of laughter one species night emerge as paradigmatic. This suggestion would allow us to study one species of laughter as paradigmatic without having to consider all possible causes, which may be innumerable and no one of which would be universal. Just as one might argue that the paradigm of courage is to be found in the warrior, and thus an existential analysis of fear, loyalty to one's own, and sacrifice, would help us understand what it means to be courageous without thereby demanding that all who have courage are warriors, so a paradigm of mirth would allow us to understand its essence without claiming a univocity of its causality. Comic laughter—by which I mean that species of laughter provoked by comedic art works—may possibly emerge as such a paradigm. One must first, however, reflect on how we do in fact make distinctions between kinds of laughter. This book is not intended as a work on laughter per se, but on comedy as a resource for truth. But as a propadeutic it is helpful to ask what it means to laugh in comedy to learn what it means to laugh at all. In order to do this, a rather simple distinction can be made solely on the basis of comparing two different ways in which we do, in fact, laugh.

Waking from his slumber following his tryst with the fairy queen, an Athenian weaver, frightened, bewildered, but still cheerful, ruminates on what he thinks was a mere dream. As his recollections sharpen, he becomes awestruck by them, and plans to ask his poet-friend, Peter Quince, to write a ballad to give artistic form to his wonder. Carried away with what he remembers, he assures us, the audience, that: "the eye of man hath not heard, the ear of man, hath not seen . . ." anything quite like what he experienced. This garbled syntax often produces at least a chuckle and sometimes a hearty laugh. But why do we laugh? Or rather: what does it mean to laugh at the solecisms of a foolish weaver beguiled by magic? The line itself is not really that funny. Do we laugh at Bottom's stupidity? But that is an unworthy thing to do, marking us as contemptuous elitists looking down with disdain on those who are so unlettered they mangle the glory of the English language. The warm, delicious joy that enables us to laugh with Bottom requires the whole play. We have, as audience, come to know and grow fond of this sanguine fellow; for there is much about his character that endears him to us. He really does not want to "affright" the ladies of the court; he is generous in his polite greetings to Titania's fairies, Peasblossom, Cobweb, and Mustardseed. Above all, he knows how to laugh at himself; so that we truly can be said to laugh with, rather than laugh at, the beguiled but goodly weaver who weaves folly and love together.

In several works, Dostoyevski offers variations of the story of a man beating his weakened horse trying to pull a cart stuck in the mud. The villagers gather round this hapless man, jeering at him and mocking his distress. Mingling shame with fury, the object of this cruel laugher continues to beat his horse with mindless, desperate savagery. As he grows more fierce, the crowd laughs all the more, pointing contemptuously at him with fingers of scorn. The circle of linked passions waxes tighter like wet rope; the more the crowd laughs, the more violent the man becomes; and the more furiously he beats his pitiful horse, the more the onlookers laugh; until finally the horse succumbs; and as he falls dead the crowd whoops triumphantly at his folly, and the man bows, bitter and defeated, all the more ashamed in the realization that he had lost not only his horse but his dignity to the petty meanness of an unworthy crowd.

Is the laughter with Bottom the same as the laughter at the Russian horse beater? They seem entirely alien, almost opposites. It is foolish for the Russian to beat his horse; for in whipping the poor animal he depletes its strength to extricate the cart from the mud. It is foolish of Bottom to say we see with our ears and hear with our eyes. In both cases, it would seem, we laugh at folly. But the nature of the laugh in the two cases is so distinct it is difficult to see them as belonging to the same species of human activity; indeed, the nature of the folly in the two cases is itself so unlike we wonder whether more is gained by distinction than by what is common.

Further, it is fairly easy to imagine or remember cases of laughter that do not appear to be enabled by folly at all. The feeble sometimes laugh at everything; the highly stressed laugh without apparent cause; the solemn will on occasion laugh uncontrollably at a funeral; the child will laugh at sheer delight, with no folly at all; the lover may laugh at the sheer, joyous ecstasy in embracing the beloved. But stress, solemnity, delight, joy, and even feeble-mindedness are not folly. If the feeble-minded and the child laugh more readily, it even seems that linking laughter to reason is suspect, for the more rational are not always the more risible. Perhaps, after all, the purely mechanistic account of laughter given by Descartes is safer, for such physiological mechanisms seem the only constant running through all these examples.

These brief reflections spot the danger of any definitionalist enterprise. A parallel can be drawn to other human phenomena. A loving husband finds his lust, not just his love, increasing as his wife responds to his erotic skills with her own heightened pleasure; *her* arousal increases *his*. The sadistic child molester finds his lust increasing as his sweet victim grows more terrified and frantic with pain. Do we say the lust is the same, but the consequences and conditions are different? Or is the sadist's lust distinct, as lust, from the loving husband's? In both cases there is arousal; but unless lust is merely that, we hesitate to identify the two. In part, this hesitation is due to what we mean by lust. If it is a certain feeling, and not a mere physical reaction, then we must stress the differences. It is rather difficult to restrict lust to reactions without any sense of the feeling that accompanies it, for when we reflect on our own lust it is often the feeling that we recall, and not the mere event. Is this nothing more, then, than the classic argument about the tree falling in an empty forest? If by "sound" we mean audial sensation, there is none; if by "sound" we mean the physical waves, there is. If by "lust" we mean only the physical arousal, both sadist and husband have the same; but if by "lust" we mean certain feelings, the two do not share the same experience.

These perils of definitional accuracy may weary the true thinker. They are genuine puzzles for lexicographers, but they are not genuine problems for a philosopher. It is important to note such denotive whimsy in language, but it is dangerous to be caught in the net of its distraction. Yet, even the definitionalist quarrels often have deeper roots. The *Oxford English Dictionary* quite rightly insists that laughter be seen always as entailing *both* the physical reactions, such as facial and abdominal shaking and the uttering of nonverbal sounds from mouth or throat, *and* the feelings or sentiments that appear to cause them. In spotting the origin of the feeling as the ludicrous, however, the *OED* reveals its Aristotelean bias. Webster does not mention the ludicrous or even the ridiculous; but refers instead to mirth and amusement. Neither mention the term *folly*. This seemingly petty quarrel reflects another side to this phenomenon. In both antique Roman and Medieval Christian literature one finds moral censure against laughter, on the grounds that it undermines *gravitas* and tends to reveal the giddy and irrational side, often conceived by Christians as the realm of Satan and by Romans the decadence of Greek culture. Certainly many of the early American Protestants were famous for their sermons condemning laughter as both frivolous and even worse, popish. It is perhaps too easy to dismiss these grim puritans as overly stern pedants; for watching today's adults convulse with ungoverned howling at the remarkably vulgar and coarse antics of a television sitcom or shriek show—I mean, talk show—gives us pause. Should we surrender our decency to the inebriate madness of the insensible? At the very least we must recognize that mindless intoxication of manic laughter may not always receive endorsement from those concerned with virtue and true joy. These reflections on the moralist's concerns, however, should at least suffice to convince us that the essence of the comic is ironically far too serious a matter to rely solely on definitions found in dictionaries or theological tracts; indeed, the issue may well be too profound to rely on any definition at all. Nor does the mere listing of possible causes offer enough. Not all who laugh, laugh well.

The praise of the comic seems more Greek than Roman; more Catholic than Protestant; more western Europe than eastern; more southern Europe than northern; though curiously, perhaps more English than Continental; more forgiving than morally correct; more divine than human, or perhaps more human than divine; more Dionysian than Olympian; more Mozartian than Beethovean; more dramatic than epic. Yet even these admittedly generalist pairings are misleading, though they may still contain a grain of truth: why does Dante call his epic a Divine Comedy? Comedy is a dramatic, not an epic, category. One might also point out some historical evidence that the rise of the comic prepares for decadence and then collapse, as Athens fell soon after Aristophanes, or as Oscar Wilde's comic genius prepared his own tragic end, and the end to the entire Belle Epoque. For the philosophical issue is not merely what constitutes the essence of the comic but what enables its praise. The latter may provide an actual, concrete phenomenon capable of being ranked, and thus make available a methodic approach to the former.

The praise of the comedic may itself be trivialized by the over-ready: laughter makes us feel good; it relieves tension, takes our minds off our failures, and enables a rather special kind of sharing, bringing us together in a most amiable way. These psychological consequences are true benefits, and it would be churlish to deny them. To focus on them as the central explanation is rather like drinking a vintage Chateau Margaux merely to experience the gentle high that follows, and not to taste its wondrous, magnificent flavor. If cheap wine also provides the same high, why ever pay so much for the vintage? It is the taste, not the high, that ranks the Margaux; it is likewise not the mere psychological benefits that endorse comedic laughter. What would it be, then? The truth, perhaps? Even if it is truth it is only that peculiarly self-revealing truth about ourselves, which may be the most important kind, but it is also the most elusive. What enables us to praise comedic laughter apparently runs more deeply than its obvious psychological benefits, and no mere suggestion of its possibility as an origin of truth suffices to justify it. Work must be done. Before we praise we must first admit the censure: the puritanic mistrust of laughter's power to enthrall us is weighty and legitimate. We may find the severity of their disapproval merely grim or even unhealthy, but they cannot be denied their point. Manic laughter, like a species of intoxication, purloins our sense and decorum, and tends to unanchor our responsibility; the parallel with drunkenness is deeply revealing. Both tend to make us irresponsible; they lower our inhibitions and restraints, making us act more like idiots than sane and dutiful citizens. There is something giddy and unseemly about the unsteady, rollicking, undisciplined antics by the victims of either toxicity, bottle, or mirth. True praise of the gifts of Bacchus is not simple endorsement: drunk drivers are a menace and should be curtailed, even severely. Manic depravity due to wanton mirth is not enviable; it can diminish or even destroy us.

The irony here, as in most matters of art and self-revelation, is the key. It is precisely that which justifies our legitimate censure that also enables our praise. We are enslaved by excesses of both vine and mirth, and slavery is almost always to be shunned. Yet, slavery to beauty, or to loyalty, or even to duty, can paradoxically and ironically, enable a deeper freedom. There are two great perils here; the first is to praise without restraint, as if no censures were legitimate and no dangers threatened; the second is to stint our praise because of the risks, as if only fulsome adulation counts, seeing in guarded endorsement a warning in disguise. What must be seen is: we censure, in such cases, for exactly the same reason we praise; and this is troubling. It is this trouble that must be embraced if truth is to be revealed.

These early, cursory remarks seem to be steered by an oceanic undercurrent, not the playful wind that puffs our sails, and that can, by seamanship, be controlled. The drift seems to pull us to narrower waters; we find ourselves speaking not of simple laughter but of a special species of it: the comic laughter wrought by comedic art. This drift, however, is not misleading. The very fact we can spot many instances of laughter that are undesirable and even unworthy shows us that, if we are to understand the phenomenon in part by praising and censuring, there is nothing wrong in letting these ruminations propel us toward that species of laughter that is self-consciously reflective. The greatest fault would be to yield to the demands of the widest generality, bringing forth a mere taxonomy of the risible. In philosophical inquiry the danger is not in leaving something out, but that in trying to include everything, only the most formal, or the bare minimalist conditions, will be gained, and that is not a gain but a loss. In seeking to understand what it means to laugh at all, it may well be that only when laughter is consciously self-reflective and self-revealing can we understand it; and comedy, as an art form, may well be not only the best, but the only, resource we have that allows us to ask in this way.

Even if we accept the strategy of approaching laughter through its art form, comedy, we must, on the warrant of caution, reflect. Not just any comedy will do. It has already been noted that those convulsed into brief idiocy by television's vulgarities are sufficiently unsavory to forfeit any praise of them. Yet, if we choose a Shakespearean masterpiece are we not offending by elitist prejudice? Restricting ourselves to the canon may warp as much as would the wanton embrace of all comic works. The need for openness and balance may seem, then, to thwart the method. To succumb to this anaesthesia of judgment is to abet the misuse of the narcotic. The analysis of a particular art work is not meant as empirical evidence to support a view, as if we were polling the laughing populace, but is rather a concrete paradigm of what can be learned about comedy from comic genius. To argue in advance that any selection must be a biased one is itself a bias, and indeed a singularly pernicious one. It is enough to note that selection itself cannot be whimsical; the reasons for the choice emerge in the analysis, and thereby become public, and as public can be challenged. To refuse to select because the choice may be vulnerable is a species of cowardice, and is unworthy of thought. We have, in our inheritance, wonderful comedies; it is stupidity not to use them. That we must select from them paradoxically reveals they may be truth-revealing, for that by which the selection is made may well be their power to reveal truth.

Men have laughed since the beginning of their history. How do we know this? Some ancient cultures have left evidence of their own laughter in varying degrees of artistic success; but not all have left remnants. Yet, this lack of evidence does not forfeit the judgment. Why? Perhaps because laughter seems native to the species: man is the risible animal. If our evolutionary origins produced nonlaughing bipeds, we might suggest they had not yet reached full humanity; for in some deep sense we seem compelled to identify laughter with our species, which is fair enough as long as we accept it provisionally. Does it follow that men have always laughed as we can laugh at Shakespeare's genius? This can be doubted. Perhaps, though we have always laughed, we have done so more in the manner of the Russian peasants in Dostoyevski's story; that is, in a crude and vulgar way; to be able to laugh with Bottom requires the highest of cultural refinement. To say we have "always" laughed may ironically suggest two things: the ability to laugh is inherent in being rational, that is, it is a fundamental characteristic of the species. But: to be able to laugh with Bottom requires long periods of cultural refinement. Since cultural refinement itself may well be also inherent in the species, this need not jar; but reflection on this possibility allows us to realize the wisdom in focusing on high art to understand the inherent enabling of laughter as native to the rational species.

If laughter truly is grounded in our ability to reason or to think, what does this suggest? Do we say: we know what reason is, and hence, our account of comic laughter must conform to how we understand our reasoning? Or might it be the other way around? We do know what comic laughter is, and since being able to reason is what enables it, we must expand our understanding of what it means to reason. If only by being rational can we laugh, then, what must be presupposed about our reasoning that may be entirely unnoticed unless and until we see it as enabling laughter, becomes a revealing question. Certainly if reason does indeed ground comic laughter, then most accounts of reasoning by philosophers are inadequate, for there is nothing in, let us say, the ability to make logic-like inferences, that would explain what happens to us when we react to the performance of a great comedy. What do we learn about reasoning if comedy is enabled by it?

A loan taken out from Plato's treasury may provide here a helpful analogue. In Book II of the *Republic* we read of Socrates providing a speculative account of the state based upon mutual advantage. The emerging *polis*, however, seems rather spartan to the youthful and eager Glaucon, who protests such a state is bereft of luxuries. When Socrates, with putative reluctance, agrees to add some, he asks Glaucon what he has in mind, and is quickly provided with several instances, including spices for food. This introduction of spices alters entirely and forever what civility offers; for now, we do not eat merely for health and life, but we dine solely because of its pleasure. Spices do not add one whit to the nutritive value of food; but they do introduce a dangerous, unhealthy, but wonderful new level of thought: I can eat, not merely to live, but simply to appreciate that I can taste at all. The whole world is changed by this introduction. In like manner, when laughter, which may be a natural instinct not unlike our desire for simple food, is refined, we then understand what it means to laugh, and not merely what causes it. Among the other luxuries added to what Glaucon contemptuously calls the pig-state, are the artists, which include the comic poets. For the Greeks this meant introducing the perilous magnificence of Dionysian spirituality, and it is from this spirit that philosophy itself emerges. And so we have a new resource for thinking about the nature of reason—not asking merely how it works and what are its criteria, but what it means to reason at all; just as spices reveal what it means to taste, rather than to eat. The Dionysian discipline that provides such self-reflective reasoning is called the love of wisdom.

It is a commonplace item of erudition that spots the Dionysian festival as the origin of drama and hence comedy. So if the inquiry into refined laughter is to be sanctioned as legitimate, its genealogy proceeding from this Greek festival cannot be overlooked. Only here, in its Dionysian genesis, can we find the true response to the question what must our reason be like if it is to sponsor comedic wisdom.

But the analogy between Glaucon's addition of spices to the *polis* and the new way of asking what it means to reason has further import. Comedy, like spiced food, no longer is in service of its product: we shift from the comic art as the cause of laughter to comic art for its own sake. For we realize that the best of artistic comedies are not at all measured by the amount of laughter they produce; at the greatest we may not laugh at all. A truly splendid production of *As You Like It*, one of the rarest few of the finest comedies ever written, may produce in lieu of laughter a warm, radiant glow of pure joy that lasts far beyond anything resembling Descartes's physiological description. Just as the finest sauce may be most appreciated when we are not hungry, so the finest comedy may be when we do not laugh. Perhaps the great comedies reveal what enables laughter without causing it, thereby accomplishing what must be true wonder rather than purpose. If this is so, the absence of laughter with the greatest of comedies is not a fault but a boon. Laughter may, in its non-cruel instances, make us feel good; not to laugh may allow us to participate, not in pleasure, but in magnificence.

If the study of comic art truly does reveal something fundamental about reasoning, we must ask further whether this revelation is due to reason itself or our humanity: that is, our being animals endowed with reason. It is a pity, in a way, that angels are no longer available for philosophic sampling, for if they were conceived as rational beings without bodies, hence without animality, we could ask: can an angel laugh? Kant, for example, insists that aesthetic judgments are not possible for purely rational beings as moral judgments are, for only with the tension and hence possible symmetry between sensibility and understanding is beauty able to be appreciated. Angels, then, would not be able to make aesthetic judgments. This suggests they probably could not laugh, either. Alas, poor angels! Perhaps it is better after all that we no longer have them in our philosophical repertoire. The question, though, persists beyond the angelic. Do we laugh because we reason, or because being human we are either cursed or gifted with both rational and nonrational faculties? Kant and Schopenhauer both seem to suggest that laughter is the result of unexpected or surprising instances of nondangerous irrationality. We can either be or witness the irrational only if we have nonrational (animalistic) faculties. This would place laughter outside the realm of reason itself, but within its purview. I laugh because my reason is shocked by my nonrational side. This is a very attractive suggestion, for it places genuine laughter within the aesthetic realm, supporting the approach that comic art is our finest resource for understanding what it means to laugh. But even if this inquiry should focus on an exploration of the comic art, how should it begin? The temptation is to reflect on the origins of this art in the Dionysian spirit of Greek thought, as Nietzsche does. This lure must be postponed, however; for the approach here is not fundamentally scholarship, but philosophy. A more felicitous technique may be to reflect on some actual comic masterpieces to see how and to what degree they succeed or fail. In this way the inquiry will be initiated concretely, for the greater danger here is that focus on contending theories may well distract us from what we need to talk about directly. By comparing actual art works in light of their comparative success and unsuccess the reality of comic learning will be directly experienced. As true masters of the dramatic craft, the Greeks initiated their dramas *in media res;* there is no reason not to follow this sage technique.

II

SILVIUS

HE is the purest lover in the forest. It is a magical place, this forest of Arden, where the very thickets are barbed with lovers; yet this poor shepherd with the golden tongue outloves them all. At his first entrance (II, 2) he shows us his scars:

> No, Corin, being old thou canst not guess;
> Though in thy youth thou wast as true a lover
> As ever sighed upon a midnight pillow:
> But if thy love were ever like to mine,—
> As sure I think did never man love so,—
> How many actions most ridiculous
> Hast thou been drawn to by thy fantasy?
>
> Into a thousand that I have forgotten.
>
> O, thou didst then ne'er love so heartily:
> If thou remember'st not the slightest folly
> That ever love did make thee run into,
> Thou hast not loved: . . .

There are our words: ridiculous, folly, sighing on a midnight pillow. We know he is stricken. More remarkable is his recognition that he is foolish and ridiculous; he bears these ascriptions as if they were honorable wounds, or awarded medals serving as badges in the office of lover. And for whom does he pine? A most unworthy Phebe, whom Rosalind warns: "Sell when you can: you are not for all markets" (III, 4). In the same passage, addressing Silvius, she asks

> You foolish shepherd, wherefore do you follow her,
> Like foggy south, puffing with wind and rain?
> You are a thousand times a properer man
> Than she a woman. 'Tis such fools as you
> That make the world full of ill-favour'd children:
> 'Tis not her glass, but you that flatters her.

Silvius makes no attempt to correct this harsh appraisal, knowing it is true; he senses that Phebe is already falling in love with the supposed boy, Ganymede, and can do nothing about it save howl in hopeless anguish, yet willing even then to serve his beloved by helping her woo his putative rival. This base fawning seems almost perverse, as if he were taking joy in being treated as a slave. Yet it is to him that even the courtiers turn to learn what it means to love. Compare the noble Orlando's silly rhymes to Rosalind with the painful, wrenching truth in Silvius's account of love when his beloved bids him: "Good shepherd, tell this youth what 'tis to love." He responds immediately: "It is to be all made of sighs and tears. . . . It is to be all made of faith and service; — . . . It is to be all made of wishes;/ All adoration, duty and obedience,/all humbleness, all patience and impatience,/All purity, all trial, all observance;—And so am I for Phebe."

In this we hear no expectation of success, no eager hope for requited passion, no ecstasy of rapture; rather, we hear only the simple facts of his sad, doting, submission. Yet, its effect on the audience is irresistible. Silvius and Phebe are the only pair entirely native to Arden; Audrey is from the forest but is wooed by the courtier's fool, Touchstone; all the other lovers are from the court. Perhaps this suggests that the simple eloquence of the locals is less entangled with art, deceit, and cunning, and therefore all the more direct. This befits Silvius's unexpected, final success: Phebe is never won over by his pitiful wooing; she yields to him solely as the result of a tricky bargain woven by the artful Rosalind. Such is the simple way country bumpkins are married, tricked into contracts they cannot escape.

What has this to do with comedy? Even if Silvius is the purest lover, he is not the central figure or even the central wooer; Orlando and Rosalind are the dramatically dominant pair; and their love is mutual; and interestingly it had been ignited prior to the shift of scenes to Arden. Silvius is not as funny as Touchstone; if we laugh at Silvius at all it is only because of his lover's plight. Indeed, his eloquence distracts from our readiness to laugh; the profundity of his love-folly is too denuding; the boy is simply too wounded to evoke much mirth. The bawdy Touchstone, feeling less, is far more available as a touchtone to laughter. Yet, without Silvius the forest would not be as magical, nor the play as we like it, nor love so revealed, nor the comedy so comic. What makes comedy comic, if Silvius can be an essential figure in *this* comic play? Some answers to this question are palpable and have already been noted: the purity of his devotion stands out, as does his simple eloquence. But there are other answers that are not so obvious and need the drama as a whole to be revealed. It is the play that shows Silvius, as lover, to be a truly comic hero.

It escapes no thoughtful reader that the most successful comedies are romantic. In art, love and laughter seem to belong together. From Aristophanes to Mozart's operas to the froth of Broadway, we laugh at lovers' folly. But not all attempts to wed the comic to the erotic are successful, and few, if any, reach the pinnacle of Shakespeare's; but even within his, the five great ones stand out: *Midsummer Night's Dream*, *Much Ado about Nothing*, *Twelfth Night*, *The Tempest*, and this one; and this one stands out even among the great five. *Midsummer* is probably the funniest, *Much Ado* the wittiest, *Twelfth Night* the most artful, *Tempest* the most magical; but this one, of all, seems to fuse love with comedy almost to perfection. One obvious point stands out: in the other four the linkage between the comic and the erotic is emphasized by the decisive separation of the clowns from the lovers. The Dogberry constabulary is distinct from Beatrice and Bendick; Bottom and his crew are set apart from the lovers in the forest near Athens; Trinculo and Stefano are quite distinct from Miranda and Ferdinand; the roguish knights Andrew and Toby are on a difference plane than Orsino and Viola. This is not to say the lovers themselves are not funny on their own; they are. But the contrast between the nonloving clowns and the loving couples obviously enhances these plays. In *As You Like It*, however, this technique is not used; and its non-use has a remarkable affect. For if the clowns and lovers are not distinct, the tendency to synthesize lover as clown and clown as lover waxes until it becomes a palpable pathos.

How do we identify this pathos? Consider these fragments as clues. We note how kindly the old man, Adam, seems, and how dearly Orlando treats him; or how gentle the old shepherd, Colin, is, even in his contests of wit with Touchstone; above all, we note how noble the exiled duke appears, making adversity sweet. When Orlando rudely interrupts his dinner of fruit and game, the Duke scolds him, perhaps already sensing the true bearing of the brash youth. The term that comes to mind is gracious. Silvius is surrounded by gracious characters, and this grace reveals and echoes that inherent in the shepherd's prostrate loving. The depth of this grace needs reflection. Adam's loyalty is remarkable: his entire life savings is readily handed over to the beloved son of his departed master, asking only that he be allowed to continue his service to the youth. His great fear is that he would die his master's debtor. This is not mere generosity wedded to loyalty—which would be rare enough: it is a bestowal based on an unselfish love; Adam's purity of devotion adumbrates Silvius's; his lonely, little soliloquy, after giving Orlando his gold, is one of the very few rhymed fragments in the whole play, setting it off as if it were a precious thing, as indeed it is. Precious as it is, though, it is matched by an equal loyalty and tenderness on Orlando's part; for the care and solicitude the boy pours out on his old servant, weakened with fatigue, hunger, and despair, are radiant. Thus, from the courtier's group seeking safety in Arden we find already in abundance the almost saint-like and generous sacrificing that bubbles up gladly from the inner depths of the soul making the characters gracious. For in each of these cases the bestowal is warmly given, rooted in a glad heart, both young and old, forest born or courtly. In no other play are so many of the characters possessed of this spiritual beauty. To understand this play one must grasp the care Shakespeare has taken in filling the stage with those possessed of grace; once we understand the centrality of the gracious we then can grasp the unique and pivotal role that Silvius has. His aching, loving, unselfish folly is the paradigm of grace, for like Adam, he gives solely from the joy of giving, "... and not for mead."

The duke manifests this grace in a manner befitting noble blood. It is not only his envied spirit in greeting adversity sweetly—though that too is echoed in Silvius's devotion—but in his magnificent greeting of Orlando. It is splendid because it reveals that the gracious is not merely passive, but ennobles by mentoring. When Orlando enters with a drawn sword, the duke remonstrates: "Art thou thus boldened, man, by thy distress:/or else a rude despiser of good manners,/That in civility thou seems't so empty" (II, 7). When Orlando blushes at the truth of this, the duke presses on: "What would you have? Your gentleness shall force/More than your force move us to gentleness." He then welcomes the youth to share his dinner, causing Orlando to reply: "Speak you so gently? Pardon me, I pray you:/ I thought that all things had been savage here; ..." He then speaks famously of the pathos of gentility, ending: "Let gentleness my strong enforcement be:/In the which hope I blush and hide my sword." Such scenes as this add a singular quality to the play found in no other; it gives Arden a magical ambiance, and ennobles the work far beyond what one might expect from a comedy. How can such grace and nobility be joined with the necessary ingredients for comedy: the foolish and the ridiculous? Even the villains in this piece are redeemed by the sacramentality of the forest. If Orlando is gracious to Adam, he is near-divinely noble in his forgiveness of his brother. Yet, we are not entirely surprised by the brothers' reunion; the play has prepared us for it. If Silvius can continue to endure his cruel enslavement, Orlando can forgive Oliver.

In the comedies, however, it is always the women and not the men who are central. Rosalind, even more than Orlando, is the commanding officer of this dramatic regiment. Yet her character, fittingly, is far more complex, even disturbing. That Silvius should see in her a rival is ironically the worst and the finest anguish for him. Were she, as Ganymede, to respond to Phebe's offering of herself, Silvius would suffer ultimate defeat, for he is no match for her. Indeed, no one in the whole play is a match for her. Yet, of all the embarrassing follies, few are as denuding as confusing the gender of one's perceived rival in love. To be defeated not by another man, but by a woman, in his suit of the unlovely Phebe, seems to mark the shepherd as inept beyond all self-acceptance. The two who love Rosalind, Phebe and Orlando, are also beguiled, but that is part of love's confusion, and hence forgivable; to be tricked in such a fundamental way by one's rival is unendurable. But nothing is unendurable to Silvius: that is his greatest folly and his greatest strength. That Rosalind turns out to be his finest benefactor, tricking Phebe into marrying him, is comic irony at its highest.

But what of Rosalind herself? If there can be a tragic flaw there can also be a comic flaw. She is dangerous. When Celia bids her to be merry (I, 2), she responds by asking: "what think you of falling in love?" Celia is quick to warn: "Marry, I pr'ythee, do, to make sport withal: but love no man in good earnest . . ." It is the most dangerous and most foolish thing suggested: we should never play with love, nor make sport with a power so awesome it can destroy us. But Rosalind is playful, perilously playful; it is part of her feminine essence. How are we to understand the great mystery of her deceit of Orlando? She is accoutered as a boy for safety's sake; but once she meets her beloved in the forest, she could have revealed herself to him; instead she continues to play at playing herself. Why? To tease Orlando? To test his love? Or is it a bit of caution in the midst of her risky playing? Or is it just pure, unadulterated fun, a singularly feminine kind of fun at Orlando's expense, conjoining danger, caution, teasing, playing, wooing, deception for its own sake, mastery of the woman over the man, folly, and no little self-deceit? Or is it her version of Orlando's confusion: "what passion hangs these weights upon my tongue?" If Phebe's direct rejection of Silvius is cruel, is not this dangerous playing with true love also cruel? Yet, in sequestration with Celia she confesses the same comic anguish over her being in love that we see in Silvius. No matter how dubious we may be about her conduct, however, she still glows, and it is this glow that seems irrepressible, wonderful, seductive, and magical. It seems, then, a more likely reading to judge the ground of her antics as a reflection of her own love-confusion than mere cunning. It fits the warmth of the play. But more importantly, it also fits its irony; for she, as the great conniver and strategist, somehow reveals herself as the most vulnerable. Her swooning at the bloody napkin is not merely another event; it reminds us of how risky and unstable her position is. We begin to realize it is not the characters in the play that make the comedy; it is comedy that enables the characters to be who they are.

The nature of this revealing itself is mirrored in Rosalind's disguise. Here is a girl pretending to be a boy, who, when she finds Orlando, pretends to be the girl she really is. If we bear in mind that in Shakespeare's day, young boys played the roles of the women, we have a boy playing a girl playing a boy playing a girl. The real, in this antic, is made available by the deceit; and that is the essence of playing: it is not, as Hamlet says, holding the mirror up to nature but holding nature up to the mirror. It is only in playful deception that we learn the truth. But to say this without the twin realization that playing is dangerous is to demote a profound truth to a banal rubric. Rosalind, as Ganymede pretending to be Rosalind, becomes a deceit that undeceives, a truthful lie, the playful as serious, the real as appearance and the appearance as real. It is only because of the all-pervading grace of the play that deception can be a means to truth. We say: Rosalind as Ganymede pretends to be herself; but in saying this we hurry past it without letting its truth matter. We must ask this profoundly: how can we *pretend* to be ourselves? We can pretend to be ourselves only if we are already in the mode of deceptive pretense. In pretending to be ourselves, is the self untrue? Certainly pretending to be oneself is not the same as being oneself. Does this mean that in playing who we are we distort our reality? Or is it the other way around: only by being able to pretend we are who we are can we discover what it means to *be* who we are? If this sounds ominous in its mendacity, a guileful trickery with words, let us first let the suggestion breathe, like fine wine poured in a glass. Suppose only by pretending to be who we are can we be who we are. If this is *true*, we must further presuppose that our very nature is to be self-deceiving; and the only way to escape from self-deceiving would be a counter-deceiving that ironically turns us back to our newly emerging reality. Rosalind, as Ganymede pretending to be Rosalind, alone can learn and disclose herself to herself.

Is this a mere formula: lying about lying is to tell the truth? The suggestion is that such formulaic reading is itself distortive: only if love—indeed love in a world of grace—is at the basis can Rosalind pretend to be Rosalind in a way that lets us (and her) see who Rosalind is in truth. And this is why Silvius is so important: for his pure, uncunning, unplaying, and direct devotion, lurking in the background, reminds us, always: the love in the forest is true love. But it is also why the sheer graciousness of most of the cast creates a spirit of such warm endorsement that we allow ourselves to learn fundamental truth by falsely pretending to be truthfully ourselves.

The little interior dramas that Rosalind and Orlando play, pretending that she is really who she is, are treasures. She "pretends" to shift her moods, being at one time coquettish, another yielding, another aloof, noting in her male guise that such is the fickle nature of women. It is only when they "pretend" to marry that both lovers begin to feel uneasy; this cuts too near the truth. What are we to make of this? Is it all mere "sport"? Or is she learning of her own feminine guile? Or is there any pretense at all? Perhaps her pretended moods are her real moods? Is she not, at the very least, mocking her own love? If so, the irony is, the more she mocks her loving, the more she loves. Silvius knowingly marks his love as both foolish and ridiculous, and in doing so loves absolutely; Rosalind mocks herself, and loves Orlando more. Is love, then, shameless? Or is it a triumph *over* mockery, even self-mockery; contrasting these lovers with the Russian who beat his horse: he became a victim of mockery, they celebrate it. And what of Orlando? He protests, "I would not be cured youth," when given the therapeutic reason for their gaming; yet, he participates in the very cure that advances rather than retards the disease. He later admits to the Duke that Ganymede reminds him of Rosalind; are we to take this as a hint that he already suspects, however vaguely, what may be the almost impossible secret? These questions tease us as we watch the play, and being teased we enjoy it all the more. In this we imitate Orlando: we allow Shakespeare to tease us as he allows her to tease him. It is "play." But just as lying about lying here reveals truth, so playing about playing reveals the serious. This may be the most serious of all serious things: learning to accept joyfully, warmfully, graciously, the dark, tearful abandonment in the harsh, cold, bitter city of folly.

If it is joy, though, we must ask if it is not a cruel deceit. If *As You Like It*, as an artwork, makes us briefly believe in joy again, then is it not an evil distraction? What right do we, denizens of the vast parking lot, have, to find joy in an illusory forest? Is it escapism? A narcotic against the clanging madness of the now-urban reality? A bit of Pollyanna to soothe our nerves? There is an escapist in the play, who rejects the merriment of the final act and seeks refuge in a monastery: Jacques. His mockery is genuine, not playful. Few scenes in all drama equal the irony of his final age of man, "sans teeth, sans taste, sans everything," providing the cue for Orlando to enter fondly carrying the old Adam. It is a simple, subtle counterpoint that is irresistible: old age on the strong back of the loving youth, contrasted by old age as mocked by scornful cynicism. Jacques has a melancholy of his own, yet even he is embraced by the warm grace of the play; he too is a comic necessity; but he provides the alternative: perhaps the entire scene of all this nuptial grace can be denounced. Rosalind's epilogue shows us we need not, and that is enough.

Reflection on this particular play as the paradigm of comedy suggests that love itself is folly, and folly is what makes us laugh. But folly itself can be warmly endorsed if it is rooted in an atmosphere of grace; and it is this graciousness that allows us to laugh at ourselves. Playing is revealed as serious: like Rosalind we can play at being ourselves, and this alone allows us to laugh with the comic lovers, not at them; and in laughing with the gentle we laugh at our own folly. There is danger here, which heightens our delight, but the risk is worth it. Indeed, not to risk is an even greater danger. As these truths deepen, however, we realize that overt laughter itself actually begins to fade as the necessary condition, for we may not laugh that much in seeing this play; it is not simply foolishness, but being foolish nobly and graciously that evokes the curious comic response, which is more akin to a rich, warm, intimate glow that comes from being able to embrace our folly; perhaps it is a smile that lasts much longer than the loud guffaws provoked by raw clowns. Or perhaps it is a species of internal laughter, all the more potent for being unexpressed. The actual label is less important than the truth revealed in the phenomenon. The comic revelation of our own truth is shown here, however, as a species of asking rather than answering. Are we foolish because we love; or are we lovers because we first are fools? If playing is always a deceit, how can deceit provide us with truth? Above all, we now must ask: what is folly? It certainly seems to have taken on a loftier status than simply doing something stupid or making a mistake because of mere ignorance. Yet, even to suggest that folly is loftier than stupidity or ignorance seems genuinely wicked and counterintuitive: to elevate folly is to cheat us of the very reason we must seek to avoid it. Is not the opposite of folly wisdom? Have we come to this outrage: it is wise to be foolish? Is it even wise to be *fond* of the foolish? At the very least there is a serious paradox here that cannot be dismissed merely by saying we enjoy comedies. Glib inversions of meaning are pernicious: property is theft; we must destroy in order to save; hate is really love; truth is untruth, decency is weakness. These slogans terrify because they are wanton; they are traps that ensnare the unwary, and must accordingly be exposed as dangerously wrong. To say it may be wise to be foolish must remain highly suspect; we cannot endorse it simply because it mocks our reason, or offends common sense. Yet, it remains a paradox and not a self-refuting contradiction. There is truth in affirming that the wise are foolish; but only if great care is take to understand it. The playful has become serious indeed.

One obvious way to defuse the seeming misology in saying the wise are foolish is to reflect on our curious suspension. We are, in fact, finite both in the extent of our comprehension and in the duration of our lives. It would be foolish and not wise to deny this. Accordingly we say that essential for human wisdom is the realization that we do not know everything, and realizing it we must come to grips with it. It does no good simply to moan and complain because we are so limited; nor does it do any good to deceive ourselves into pretending we really do know all that is important and worth knowing, or that technology and science will eventually answer all questions. Thus, we say, it is wise to admit we are unwise. This account seems banal on its surface: indeed, as stated it is banal. However, when we seriously reflect on our suspension between knowing everything and knowing nothing, a curious thing may happen. The truth of that suspension itself becomes unexpectedly rich in its meaning. We seem to exult in this self-discovery, realizing that being in the middle is somehow wondrous or thrilling. Such realization need not happen, of course; some may find our suspension a cause of anger, self-despising, or even blatant misology. But these negative reactions seem somehow noncompelling, perhaps even misguided. Can we, should we, exult in our finitude? The play *As You Like It* shows us we can; and in showing us we can exult, we learn the new kind of wisdom that endorses our folly. This in no longer a mere abstract reflection on the impoverishment of our epistemic exchequer; it is a concrete, palpable realization of what it means to be able to be foolish without disdaining or hating the folly within us. This realization is the key. How do we, in confronting our imperfection, avoid self-hatred and self-mockery? The laughter at the hapless Russian beating his horse disdains our folly; the response to Shakespeare's play endorses it. If human wisdom be the goal of philosophy, the understanding of how comedy saves us from the misology of hating our finitude must emerge as one of our most compelling tasks. What may at first seem a small subdivision of the least respectable of all philosophical endeavors, aesthetics, becomes instead a critical, ontological necessity. We must learn how it is wise to be foolish; and only great comedy provides the erudition. We no longer ask simply how, why, or what it means to laugh; we now realize that we ask about our reality as foolish and wise; and if Shakespeare's comedies are a resource, we find being wise and foolish at once is enabled only by lovers being fools.

We cannot forget that these discoveries are accomplished by reflecting on an actual, performed play. If the drama enables us to think about our suspension, the very craft of the playwright must be noted. The success of this play has been identified provisionally as grace. If it is the gracious that gives to this particular comedy the envied status of a paradigm, the question then becomes: is grace necessary for comedy, at least for comedy as a resource for truth? Most of Shakespeare's comedies possess the gracious to some extent. This may be due to the dramatist's own gentle nature, attested to by his contemporaries; or it may be due to the profound influence of Christianity's emerging emphasis on forgiveness; it may be due as well to the rising spirit of the Renaissance, or to Elizabeth's charismatic rule. It may also be due to the simple maturing of the art form itself. The possible influences are almost endless; perhaps they all play a role. Regardless of the social causes, there is a spirit in all of Shakespeare's comedies that is easily identified as gracious. But, if grace is part of the *craft* by which this particular wright accomplishes success, is it not false generality to suggest grace may be essential for comedy? Furthermore, one might argue it is not love as enabling grace that is central, but lust. Perhaps what is foolish is simply the silly things one gender does to mate with the opposite gender. If this is the case, it is not grace-enabling love that makes the comedy, but the silliness of putatively rational beings yielding to their carnality. Shakespeare's addition of kindly grace to the play would, if this were true, make it more charming, "nicer" perhaps, but not a paradigm of the comic.

To test whether grace and love may be nonessential, replaced perhaps by lust, it is perhaps fitting to change the venue of the search.

III

CHERUBINO

THE youth, as the libretto tells us, is at that supremely dangerous age: young enough to be given liberties, just old enough to take improper advantage of them. His voice is yet soprano, but there are hints of the emerging male; he is utterly charmed by the ladies, but being sweetly young, he also charms them; and his successes amaze even as they confuse him. He seems to flirt by instinct, wearing the mask of innocence, trusting utterly that no lady would ever betray his conquests. He is a naughty boy. Yet, when he sings his own little song, which he wrote, *voi che sapete*, asking whether those who know what love is can tell him if he, suffering yet joyous, is a lover, not only he, but the whole global populace of lusting sinners seems utterly forgiven. Music of that power, genius, and creamy voluptuousness, truly beyond compare as only the rarest achievement of art can produce, unfangs all the tigers of moral censure and leaves us breathless, as if denuded of virtue, yet totally redeemed. If his is a dangerous age, the music he sings is dangerous art. A central, recurring technique of this aria consists of a single high note followed by a single low note, and this descent is repeated as if an echo of itself; these twin descents are then themselves repeated in a lower, richer register, and reiterated in different keys. The melody surrounding these paired descents is almost silky with richness of sonority, both merry and light, but plucking at chords that suffer and agonize, producing a sense of wondrous self-wonder. The beauty of this three-minute aria is of haunting penetration; hearing it once it is ours forever; but even at first it is already curiously familiar, as if we had always known it, incorporate at our birth; but at every hearing it is entirely new, stunning with its freshness. We hear the boy aching for love, mindless of its impropriety, and yield to the tortured sweetness of his longing. Written in 1785, it yet adumbrates the highest romanticism, as if no mere label denoting a period is adequate. Mozart was still in his twenties when he wrote *Le Nozze di Figaro*; but in his boyhood he, too, was a charmer of the ladies, as much a prodigy in flirtation as in music. Perhaps Cherubino is the young Mozart: he knew whereof he wrote. Even those who prefer Wagner and Verdi, exulting in the great crescendos and full-chorus fortissimi, nevertheless yet yield to this flawless, perfect, most human in being unhuman, bit of comic opera. The absolute beauty of *voi che sapete* transcends all descriptions.

Therein, however, is the greatest philosophical danger. We are tempted to say the rarity of its musical beauty is why we listen to it. It has nothing to do with comedy or the eighteenth century or boys in love with older women or even morality or immorality; it is simply a pure, aesthetic experience, a melody loved by many who do not even know it comes from an opera. Perhaps the reflections on Shakespeare's *As You Like It* are also irrelevant: it is the beauty of his poetry, we might say, that lures us to the play; the drama is a mere vehicle to poetic beauty, just as the opera is a vehicle to musical beauty. There is no doubt we can happily listen to the poetry shorn of the drama; just as we happily listen to the music shorn of the silly plot. The fact that Mozart as musician and Shakespeare as poet may, in their art, achieve autonomous lures to listen to them is true enough, but it does not follow the drama is irrelevant. We may even suggest that, though I may listen to *voi que sapete* played on a piano merely as music, it is better to hear it in the opera, because in the drama *as* drama it is truly more beautiful. Watching the whole opera allows us to learn from this aria a part of Cherubino's character and the universality of his comic anguish. The music itself, then, and not the mere libretto, is dramatic. Nevertheless, this dangerous possibility that poetic and musical beauty are independent of the drama is a serious problem; it is serious because it is true that the beauty of the music and the poetry can be appreciated independently of the drama; but it is also true that such beauty belongs in the drama; indeed, even when played or recited independently, it is still dramatic beauty. There is something of a paradox here, that needs working out.

Da Ponte's libretto is taken from Beaumarchais's play, which was censored by the Emperor Joseph II, giving some difficulty to the opera's performance. The comedy is of a familiar genre: it deals with infidelities, jealousy, cruel tricks to catch the sinners in the act, or to force by blackmail the wanderer back to his proper bed. It is a bawdy, bedroom farce, winking at adulterous liaisons and apparently mocking the solemnity of marital vows. The final act borders on vaudeville: who hides where? Who cheats on whom? The whole spirit of the plot is mistrust and suspicion, all the more venal for being warranted; the final triumph at the end does little to assure us any of the lovers will not stray again. The plot, then, seems entirely lacking of the warm grace found in Arden; it is closer to the mean-spirited, almost cruel comedy of the ancient Greeks.

It is the music, though, that accomplishes and reveals the grace. However, it is not gracious music added on to a graceless plot, but music that delves beneath the surface of all-too-human characters and reveals to us who they are; and within their characters can be found, not simple or pure grace, but grace struggling with banality, making it all the more powerful. *Voi che sapete* delivers to us a Cherubino the plot alone could not: we hear in its denuding beauty what it is like to be a boy on the threshold of manhood, lusting as a part of his nature after the feminine, but in that carnal phenomenon is found in *this* boy, love, not mere lust; and it is the authenticity of that love that surprises him—for surprise or awe is at the essence of those four-note descents. The sweetness of the aria's central theme is richened with the tonality of reverence; and reverence is not a quality of lust but love. Why should we object to music playing this dramatic role, especially since it works? Why should a green boy's lust not bring forth true love, as long as the boy has it within him to feel the sweet slavery of genuine longing? It is love, not mere lust, that confuses. If this depth is achieved only by the music, then why not admit the music is fundamentally a part of this drama, and not a mere ornament added as an afterthought? Beaumarchais may not agree, but audiences hearing the opera know it is true.

The same can be said for Shakespeare's poetry. That we can appreciate it on its own does not forfeit our realization that the blank verse in *As You Like It* enables us to dig more profoundly into the anguish of Silvius, which then serves as an access to the more important anguish of Rosalind. There is a parallel between Silvius and Cherubino that transcends their mere youthful love agonies. Neither are dominant characters; yet to clepe them "minor" roles is artistic felony. Figaro, Susanna, and the Countess sing far more notes than Cherubino; Rosalind and Orlando have far more lines than Silvius; these artworks cannot be said to be "about" these two lovesick boys. Yet it is their characters that provide almost unfathomable depths to both dramas, characters revealed only by the most beautiful artistry. In a way, both boys, being so young and hence so vulnerable, possess a kind of innocence that somehow assures both audiences that courtly art, though dangerously trivial, can be rooted in less artful, more authentic, character; but ironically, this truth is learned only by the finest art of all. Without these befuddled youths we would tend to forget how honest the agony of love can be. Underlying the frivolity of these dramas is a deep respect for the institution of marriage; we cannot forget the title of Mozart's work, nor the entrance of Hymen in the final act of Shakespeare's play.

Da Ponte's script, after all, is less explicit than it may first seem. Cherubino was found hiding in Barbarina's bedroom, which in those days and circumstances was naughty enough; perhaps he succeeded in seducing her. In art, the implicit is far more important than the explicit; our imagination is brought into play with wonderful effect. Lustful love is still love; perhaps for boys like Cherubino the distinction is not clear at all. It may be an essential part of his innocence not to discern the difference; this uncertainty imbedded in his innocence finds truth-revealing resonance in the script's ambiguity, intensified by the musical ambiguity found in key changes, especially the shifts from major to minor, but also in the more subtle changes in tonality. Those dissatisfied with the ambiguity of art, who insist they should know exactly what goes on so they can judge this opera either as a liberal endorsement of enlightened promiscuity or as puritanic censure of antisacramental licence, misread and hence misguide. The ambiguity is not a tease; it is a truth. Do any of us ever know the exact demarcation between lust, eros, and marital love? Do we want to know? We know the difference; we *must* know the difference; we need not, perhaps cannot ever know, the demarcation. Perhaps we are in the middle again: not only between wisdom and folly but between love and lust. Perhaps it is this romantic and musical ambiguity that is our own fundamental truth. Cherubino sings this truth, not only in *voi que sapete* but perhaps more accurately in the earlier, and equally, perhaps surpassingly, beautiful *Non so pìu cosa son, cosa faccio*. He, certainly, at least, *is* in the middle; and being there is intensely painful and intensely wonderful.

Because of his indiscretion at being found in Barbarina's bedroom, the Count punishes him—and not incidentally, to get him out of the way—by sending him to the regiment. The army is the one place this happily lovesick boy does not belong. We ache at the suggestion: this boy is designed for love, not killing. But even if the regiment never goes to battle, the coarsening of barracks life might well change the entire nature of Cherubino's approach to women; he will learn there to fulfill his already remarkable appetite for the feminine in a manner designed to gratify, not fill him with awe. Accordingly, we the audience desperately do not want this to happen, and are relieved when the Count is stymied by failing to seal the order. Yet this added touch touches a deeper matter. Cherubino will grow up, just as Silvius will. Will he become another Count? A Don Giovanni? A Figaro? The boyish innocence and naughtiness is necessarily a fleeting thing, as is the whole magic of these plays. They are all the more precious for that; though happily we can always go back and see them again, where they are fresh as ever. In this sense art is a cheat on nature, but not on truth. Actual boys grow up; true ones, as *true*, remain who they are.

The question whether lust or love is laughed at in comedy turns out to be far more serious than it may at first seem. We can indeed laugh *at* the hijinks taken by the genders to come together even among nonhuman animals; we laugh *with* lovers fretting with the restrictions of custom and the aching realizations of duty, responsibility, and awe-struck enslavement emerging from the feral lust of youth. It is the art of comedy that changes our laughing at to laughing with, until the latter may become a silent, gracious joy. This shift is aided by the operatic: though we may laugh at some irresistible comic moments during the opera, we hesitate to mar the glorious music with our own noise. So beautiful is the score we feign would not laugh at all than disturb its magical power on us. We find it especially irksome if others in the audience drown out this beauty with sustained guffaws. This de-emphasis of actual laughter reflects the comedic shift from "at" to "with," from amused satisfaction *at* the folly of others to the tacit thrill of bemused learning of truth *with* the comedic mirroring of our own folly.

Emerging from these concrete reflections on actual characters in real dramas are several important discoveries, which perhaps now should be noted before our asking reaches deeper levels. Numbers may help, though they seem pedantic. 1) Mozart's music and Shakespeare's poetry are themselves dramatic, and not merely decorative additions to the drama. 2) We laugh *at* the folly of lust but laugh *with* the folly of love. 3) For both the play and the opera, grace emerges as that quality that enables us to laugh with rather than at. 4) We do not laugh with the merely lustful nor with the sacramentally pure fidelity of marriage, but only with the erotically tormented. 5) To the question, are we amused at lovers because they are foolish or fools because they are lovers, we can provisionally suggest: if laughter is the target, we answer: we laugh at fools and all lovers are foolish; if comedy is the target, we answer: we laugh with lovers, and some fools are lovers. This last point ranks comedy above laughter, and deserves further reflection. But it is the first point that should be developed now, since forgetting it abuses the entire inquiry, particularly in the focus on Cherubino.

The history of music itself is revealing, and even ironic. For most of its tenure, music was itself more supportive than independent. In Western culture, it served four important institutions. The first, and by far the greatest, was the Church. Masses, psalms, requiems, *Te Deums* and ecclesiastical pomp were all supported by music, some of it glorious. Even for as late a figure as Bach, church music dominated his portfolio. If one wanted to be a musician, one went to the ecclesiastical authorities; who else, besides kings, could afford it? Even Wagner sought a post as *Kappelmeister*. Mozart, Beethoven, Schubert, and Brahms wrote Masses and Requiems long after music had reached its autonomy. Second only to the church was the army. Martial spirit is enhanced by martial music, even if reduced to fife, drum, and bugle. Marches stir the soul, and some good music can be found in this service to the king's favorite necessity. As society began to recover from the ravages of darkness, the kingly courts also provided the third institution supported by "incidental music," played to establish a certain degree of refined decorum or courtly behavior. Mozart himself wrote pieces he called "divertimenti"—though his transcend that lowly title. The fourth supported institution was drama. Opera, as we know it today, had more humble beginnings; earlier, music simply accompanied the action, thereby providing it with an older history than what came to be known as "absolute music," that is: music conceived as high art heard solely for its own sake, especially symphonies, concertos, and sonatas. Curiously, however, the ascendency of these so-called absolutist forms, concertos, sonatas, and symphonies, themselves brought to autonomous heights by none other than Mozart, deepened their contribution to opera. Music in opera became not a mere service or enhancement to the centrality of plot and character, but an essentially dramatic art on its own. Drama itself, in maturing, had shifted from plot to character, especially in comedy, and operatic music became a resource first in refining character, but then as an autonomous element in drama as such. To a great extent, this elevation of the *dramatic* nature of music was achieved also by the genius of Mozart. But it was given theoretical authority by no less a titan than Wagner himself, who argues in *Opera and Drama* that all music, even and especially the heights of absolute music, such as Beethoven's Third and Ninth Symphonies, is still dramatic at its core. Drama is male, Wagner argues, and music female. The philosopher Schopenhauer, on whom Wagner heavily relied, provides profound reasoning for this attribution. Music is dramatic in part because it deals directly with the passions, and passion is the essence of drama. If music is the closest art to the passionate will, and drama is the articulation of passions, the wedding of these two art forms is not incidental, and certainly not distracting; rather it is inevitable. Indeed, the proximity of poetry to music may even be seen in the high success of poetic drama; we use Mozart to learn about Shakespeare.

The paradox is that the achievement of absolute music actually reinforces its dramatic essence. To say the arias of Cherubino reveal him to us in a way the mere story cannot is now grounded in profound philosophical reflection.

The second discovery, that we laugh *at* the folly of lust and *with* the folly of love is not a mere insight; it, too, has philosophical significance. In *The Risk of Being* I offered a suggestion that may prove helpful here: we can call what is laughed *at* the silly, and what is laughed *with*, the foolish; both the foolish and the silly constitute folly in the broader sense. In that book, however, the distinction was made to facilitate the analysis of judgment; here it is simply in service of our understanding of comedy: we can call the antics of lust silly and the torment of love foolish. With this suggestion the foolish are clearly more loveable than the silly, and the nature of our comedic response to the silly is thus less gracious, perhaps even flavored with ridicule; hence, the ridiculous. Nevertheless, it would be grossly inappropriate to excise the silly from the legitimate venue of comedy. Indeed, within a single great comedic work the very contrast is enlightening: we may call Malvolio in *Twelfth Night* silly and Viola foolish; or in the present case, we might say the Count is silly, Cherubino foolish. In comedy we find ourselves reflected in both the silly and the foolish, but the natures of such reflections are vastly different: it is the aesthetic distance from silliness that redeems, for being silly is in fact morally dangerous; it is our embrace *of* foolishness that affirms our finite humanity. Being exposed as foolish is humbling, but without a loss of worth; being silly is arrogant, and its exposure tends to make us resentful, even revengeful. Great comic artists can weave these two modalities of folly together to huge effect not only within a single drama, by sketching one character as foolish and the other as silly, but even more remarkably by wedding then in a single, complex character. The antics of Falstaff, for example, may be both; and perhaps even the Count in *Figaro*, or, more ominously, Don Giovanni, may be silly and foolish, allowing us both to affirm and to censure. Cherubino and Silvius, however, are foolish, not silly; and that is their glory. The puritans, Malvolio in *Twelfth Night* and Angelo in *Measure for Measure*, are entirely silly, and not foolish; yet they properly belong in these two great comedies.

The nature of folly itself, which includes both the silly and the foolish, now emerges as a question of utmost concern; but it deserves its own chapter. For the present, it is enough to suggest that what constitutes the difference between the silly and the foolish in comedy is the spirit of grace that enables the latter; and thus provides access to the third discovery. Grace is the thematic center of *As You Like It*; but in Mozart's opera it is the musical center—bearing in mind that music here is a dramatic, and not mere tonal, art. How are we to understand this? Whatever else grace means, it is nondeserving. Like folly, grace deserves its own analysis; but we already have enough to suggest its import. If the gracious is bestowal not based on desert but on favor, we see the power of its role in comedic art. The gracious is enabled, not by our moral worth, for that establishes rights and duties, but our existential worth, in which who we are matters more than what we do. Cherubino learns this from both sides: there is something in his nature that bestows, even if it is simply his own gracious charm—we may even say he bestows himself. Unlike the merely lustful who only take, he gives; and this giving is not on the basis of desert, but favor. Yet, the boy also is bestowed, and he knows this. The favors, however illicit, given him are as gifts, not rights nor extortion. The richness of this two-sided graciousness, both giving and receiving as bestowals, is palpable in the dramatic music. From this musical bestowal we learn the truth of grace itself. Few experiences in the entire universe are as gracious as listening to Mozart: we surely do not deserve its favor, yet it is given in such grace we take joy in being grateful.

The fourth discovery intensifies this sense of being-in-between. The foolish need not occur in simple lust, though silliness might; nor in marital ecstasy, but in that far more troubling species of loving known as the erotic. The god Eros is profoundly praised in Plato's *Symposium* and *Phaedrus*; and there is an entire literary tradition given over to the reverence and study of this Dionysian element in our spirituality. The key to its importance is the link it provides between body and soul, man and god, reason and sense. Eros has a divine father and a mortal mother, knows the carnal yearnings of the wanton profligate as well as the noble sacrifice of the committed spouse, enslaves as it liberates and frees as it enthralls. It is thus profoundly paradoxical, and in its artistic expression is almost always ironic. In Cherubino's case we see it as an essential part of beauty and youth; yet it cannot charm without some sense of danger. It is not obsession, for that may be entirely carnal, lacking any spirit whatsoever, and may corrupt us entirely, or even kill us, as we learn from Therese Raquin. The erotic may on occasion be obsessional, but it is probably truer to describe it as enslaving, or in its literal sense, enthralling.

We may gain much from listening to Cherubino. In scene 5, Act I, we hear the rapid protest: *non so pìu cosa son, cosa faccio . . . /or di foco, ora sono di ghiaccio* ("I do not know what I am or what I do; Now I burn, now I shiver . . ."). That the tempo here is so hurried suggests both impatience with himself at getting his message out, and the breathlessness inherent in his confusion. His sudden, impulsive repetition of *Ogni donna mi fa palpitar* ("every woman makes me tremble") intensifies his vulnerability. The sonority deepens and the tempo slows at *solo ai nomi d'amor* ("at the very word, love, I tremble"). The modulation ripens even further, with a rich, rolling luxurious sensuousness at *Parlo d'amor vegliando* ("I speak of love when I'm awake")—then thickens further like simmering chocolate on the stove, at the next line *Parlo d'amor sognando* ("I speak of love when I sleep"). When he sings of love to the very echo and the wind *All'eco all'aria, ai venti*, the music itself becomes positively wavy, like the wind itself, rustling the leaves in musical swimming. It ends *Es se non ho chi m'oda/Parlo d'amor con me* ("And if no one hears me, I talk about love with myself"), in sad, slow, lonely measures; the music now hushed, gentle, and somber. Obviously the boy is in love with women, not only this or that woman, which allows us to realize his is not quite the fullness that Figaro has for Susanna, and certainly not what the Countess has for the undeserving Count. Yet, it is not obvious that he is *merely* in love with love—that is a part of it, to be sure—but the music shows that he loves them, not only it—the beloved and not mere love itself.

The extent to which the boy's indifference to propriety indicts, however, must be shared in part by the women. After all, Susanna and the Countess are more mature than he, yet they not only wink at his transgressions but seem to abet them. In the case of the Countess, the boy is treading on grounds of high peril and impropriety, perhaps even *lèse majestè*: he aches for a woman far above his station. By their amusement, if not their participation, Cherubino is led to believe love truly can wink at all propriety with impunity. When genuine peril threatens him in the Countess's bedroom, the two ladies assist him in escaping in part because they realize their own moral delinquency in playing such dangerous games. They did not serve him well in their moral lapse. Someone ought to have scolded him earlier as Figaro does later. But so sympathetic is his lover's plight and gracefully charming his character that the audience itself endorses the women's misdemeanor, almost, but not quite, forgetting that their support of his erotic folly nearly cost him his life and themselves their own happiness.

Eros is confusing, sad and joyous, dizzy and sobering; unlike spousal love it can be of many or of one; unlike mere lust it does not satisfy but waxes our longing; the more we surrender to it the more it enslaves us; yet the more we try to extricate ourselves from its chains, the more wretched we become. So we are fools if we yield and fools if we do not. Few may be so captive as Cherubino, but even fewer are entirely unfamiliar to its ache. But if it treats us so dismally, why do we enjoy it in the warm, internal laughter that is provoked by this folly? The fifth discovery re-emerges again as an asking: is it the foolish as lovers or the lovers as foolish that embrace us in this profane sacrament of joy? In comedy, it seems we embrace lovers as fools; laughter's targets are the fools who happen to love. But even if this latter is less worthy, it still belongs as an important part of comedy, and provides an interesting analogue to it.

Laughter, like yawning, is contagious. We are often led to join in even if we do not know its origin: we laugh at laughing. Or: we may smile while reading a comic play; but seeing it performed before a ready audience, we laugh, now, at the same line that provoked only the smile at reading. There are many reasons for this, including the possibility that those convulsed by mirth simply look ridiculous, causing us to join in against our will. There is though, unlike the contagion of yawning, a communal power in the phenomenon; it brings us together in a wondrous way, eroding the insular differences that may bar us from sharing a passion together. Laughter, briefly, unites us; when this uniting is accomplished by high art, the ensuing community is a polity of grace. Sharing a tragedy may intensify our uniqueness; we may feel marooned in our shock, and want to be left alone; but comedy joins us in an ensemble of folly-generated delight; we seem more inspired to talk immediately after a comic than a tragic play. This unifying contagion is supremely echoed in operatic art by means of the ensemble, unsurpassed in *Le Nozze di Figaro*. The last twenty minutes of the second act is virtually one long, wondrous, almost incredible, feat of ensemble singing, involving eight different voices, in seeming ease, bringing forth the comic resolution. Since this is something only operatic comedy can do, it deserves reflection.

The ensemble may seem the essence of high musical art, whether in a string quartet, a symphonic fugue, or an operatic triumph such as the quartet in *Rigoletto*. To hear many voices or musical lines woven together in a tapestry of polyphony seems among the finest of art's offerings; counterpoint thrills us in part because each individual voice becomes ironically more distinctive, yet the overall weaving together produces a unity that is an independent phenomenon enjoyed on its own. So we hear both each and all at the same time, taking from this mixture of the one and the many a singular delight that reflects our own mystery of being one in a manifold universe. In Mozart's comic opera, however, the effect is extraordinary, for the anguish of love is universalized even as it individualizes, giving a palpable and concrete insight into the deepest paradox of our existence: who are we as self and species? Who are we as lover and as love? If spousal love unites two as one, comic love, by the art of the ensemble, unites the many as one.

Mozart is said to have considered the vast ensemble that is the finale of Act II to be his own favorite, his greatest masterpiece. Whether this is actually true, it certainly deserves to be among the contenders. The musical ensemble has no peer in other arts; syntheses of worthy parts into worthier wholes can occur in almost all art, but not as concretely as in a drama, where different personalities and different moods are braided together into a unifying theme; but even poetic drama is limited by the fact that three actors saying different lines at the same time is unhearable. Absolute music weaves several musical threads together in fugues and counterpoint; but only opera can do this both musically and dramatically at once.

The Count believes his wife is having an illicit romance with the boy, Cherubino, who lurks hiding in the closest, his "chest bare," his wife admits, because he was being dressed as a woman. But it is not Cherubino but Susanna who emerges; the boy had escaped jumping out the window. This farcical situation, however, is an opportunity for deep disclosures: the Count is jealous and angry; then befuddled and outwitted; the Countess is first imploring, then censuring her husband for mistrust, then plaintive in her longing to be trusted; Susanna is witty, loving, contemptuous of the Count's desires yet soothing him in his ire. In the two women we hear the quality of true devotion, love as pure as the Count's is not, constant as the Count's is frail. All these passions are musically supported; to hear them all at once, or at least interwoven in altering sequences, unifies them as a vast tapestry of folly—but folly entirely charmed by musical grace, bringing all these conflicts together. The jealousy of the Count is still jealous, but it becomes grounded in his genuine love for his wife, making it both unified with and in contrast to, the overall harmony of the whole.

The ensemblic synthesis curiously reminds us of philosophical inquiry itself: to avoid contradiction, we make distinctions; but hurriedly and badly made distinctions can result in incoherence—how do we re-join Descartes's radically distinct body with the soul?—requiring that distinctions greatly made paradoxically enhance coherence, unifying them in highest thought. This is inquiry at its highest level. It is concretized in the operatic finale: jealousy is mistrust; true love is trustful, music first separates them, then unites them; individuals are distinct, perhaps most distinct in art; yet in art, they become mirrors of the universal, the whole is seen in the part. The ensemble brings trust and mistrust, love and revenge, cunning and submission, confusion and learning, wisdom and folly, together; not just conceptually together but palpably together. It is *felt* as one, enjoyed as one, but heard also as many. If Kant is correct in his claim that synthesis is the essence of thought, then this operatic finale is thought *heard*. Yet, it is not merely a heard, and hence palpably concrete, musical synthesis, it is also a singularly *comic* synthesis. To understand this, further reflection on what actually happens may contribute to our understanding.

The situation is truly dire. The Count is in a jealous rage, and Cherubino's very life may be forfeit. Were the shirtless boy found in the bedroom, the Countess would be judged an adulteress. Jealousy is a perilous pathos, and for a man as short-tempered as the Count, possibly lethal. The boy's leaping out a window may seem drastic; but it is far less risky than confronting the Count as his wife's putative seducer. The dust of tragedy always hangs on the skirts of comedy; and this situation is suspenseful even to a frequent visitor. Yet, if tragedy is the development from light to dark, comedy is from dark to light; and these truly dark threats become lightened escapades through the power, not of the sheer fortuity of the giddy plot, but of the characters involved, and it is the truth of these characters that emerges musically in the grand ensemble. For this is what we hear all at once: the Countess shifts from trepidation to relief, relief to scolding, and scolding to the deepest devotional love of them all; courage on the part of Cherubino, Susanna, and above all the Countess, triumphs over surrender, and this emergence of valor is musically felt. The Count transforms himself from rage to outrage, to shock, and then to puzzlement, and finally to an enforced apology, realizing that the root of his jealousy is his love for his wife; Susanna's trust in her own fidelity and wit also encourages. The ensemblic whole, however, itself now a concrete reality as we hear it, irresistibly transforms us from peril to suspense, from pathos for the Countess, to joy at the triumph of right and beauty over wrong and ugliness. The music, as ensemblic, nevertheless unfolds into a gathering crescendo, giving a gracious triumph to what began as an ungracious menace.

Curiously, perhaps, the ensemblic finale, though it brings about a wondrous resolution within the plot, is actually a greater weaving of character than of circumstances. This point needs reflection. Good writers, or perhaps more tellingly here, good teachers of writing, know that what distinguishes the great from the merely good in the arts of narrative and drama is the development of character; plot development is inferior in importance to this. Herman Melville tells us that if one wants to write a mighty book one must have a mighty theme; but this is a warning against triviality; in his own art Melville shows it is character, not theme or plot, that ranks. Comic themes and plots may be light indeed, but if the characters within them are skillfully drawn, the theme is shown to be less frivolous and hence worthier. It is not an unworthy theme to show the triumph of true love over jealousy; but it seems a vulgar point if made solely on the serendipity of a fortuitous plot, or if it rests on vapid characters that neither grow nor even act coherently. The history of the various theatrical and narrative arts shows that as an art matures, so does the reliance on character. Morality plays are meant to teach us a lesson; for them, plot and theme are dominant. But as artistic refinement developed simple morality plays into tragic and comic masterpieces, the centrality of character became established.

There is a paradox here: one might assume that themes are more universal than plots, and plots more universal than characters, for characters are unique. Art, however, reverses this order of universality: the more profoundly refined the character, so that there is only one Hamlet or Lear or even only one Cherubino, the more universal he becomes. Here universality does not mean generality, but understandability: only as unique and concrete is Cherubino or Hamlet understandable, and only as uniquely understandable is his universality rendered concrete. The weaving of voices in ensemble singing emphasizes the universal in the concrete, in part by contrast, but in greater part by the establishment of a palpable, *felt* coherence bringing together the many variables concretely in the music itself. The ensemble, wonderfully and ironically, as it unifies, lets emerge all the more clearly the individual character. This Mozart does beyond any other artist. Yet, his is magnificently a comic art. If laughter as a social phenomenon is contagious, establishing a gathering of the many into one, comic art gathers the many into one as ensemblic, and the result is breathtaking. Yet, as it redeems, it seems to slight the authority of the moral, and this remains a serious danger. That danger must now be considered more fully.

IV

Lord Goring

OSCAR Wilde's play *An Ideal Husband* may seem an uneasy selection. It is not of the artistic perfection of Shakespeare's play or Mozart's opera; and there is a touch of decadence in any of Wilde's major works that gives us pause. His death in 1900, the same year Nietzsche died, marked the last phase of that overtly bright but covertly dark period of *la Belle Epoche*; a period characterized by the emergence of the aesthete, with its dandyism, corruption, and early nihilism. This play itself is a symptom; because of Wilde's trial and conviction, it was yanked from the London stage and was almost forgotten for generations; it seems to reek of the personal corruption associated with its author and its doomed epoch. Yet, it is precisely this association, however unfair, that suggests this play to be considered; for comedy, must, in order for it to achieve its divine significance, skirt the dangers of decadence, a species of corruption that enables the comic to be seen as redemptive. Shakespeare's play was soon followed by the grim, unsmiling revolution wrought by the moral puritans; Mozart's opera was soon followed by the equally grim Terror of the French Revolution; Wilde's play was followed by a puritanic Armaggedon. We are most corrupt when, like Robespierre, we are incorruptible.

If this vast and dubious sweep of history seems an entirely unwarranted burden placed upon a simple, witty play that scarce figures in the canon, the reasoning is nevertheless telling. Comedy confronts corruption.

One might be doubtful of the historical parallels, for it could just as easily be argued that the great comedies do not so much presage the coming collapse, but crown the brilliance of the precedent age; or one could even argue that both readings contain some truth, thereby weakening the impact of either; or perhaps indeed there is no significance at all: genius is whimsical as to the age it selects, and we should be content that it visits us at all, regardless of the calendar. The parallel therefore need not be seen as causal; but to deny causal connection between the art works and the variations of epochs does not keep one from spotting an isomorphism in their existential meaning. We are, both historically and as mirrored in comic art, capable of corrupt decadence and the redemptive salvation from it. That parallel alone suffices.

As is the case in the Shakespearean and Mozartian comedy, the figure chosen for consideration is not the focal character in the plot: Sir Robert Chiltern and his wife are; but he is a dominant player; far more than either Silvius or Cherubino. Lord Goring at first appears a deliberately shallow, foppish aesthete, like Wilde himself, proud of his own insouciance and mockery of the serious. He even instructs his butler, "For the future a more trivial buttonhole, Phipps, on Thursday evenings" (Act III). What could it possibly mean to want a more *trivial* flower for his lapel? What would a trivial flower look like? The suggestion is hilarious. A pleasure reserved only for readers of the script is Wilde's description of him at his first entrance:

> Thirty-four, but always says he is younger. A well-bred, expressionless face. He is clever, but would not like to be thought so. A flawless dandy, he would be annoyed if he were considered romantic. He plays with life, and is on perfectly good terms with the world. He is fond of being mis-understood. It gives him a post of vantage.

Who would expect from such a dandy the depth of character and loyalty to friend that emerges in the drama! Yet, it is the very unlikelihood of this nobility that is crucial to the play and to Wilde's comic genius. As in the other two dramas, it is precisely the richness of character development that sustains the greatness of the art. Wilde, more self-consciously than Shakespeare or Mozart, plays upon the seeming contradiction between the surface and the depth, finding much of his comedic art in the inversions from one to the other. Deceit becomes honesty, the trivial becomes serious, the decent indecent, the weak strong, the selfish altruistic, the disloyal loyal. These inversions serve art extremely well, but seem to disserve morality. Such playing with deceits roils the conscience, fills us with doubt about morality, and possibly even scandalizes the vulnerable, sapping the strength of rectitude and duty. Bawdy and vulgar comedy does not do this, and hence paradoxically is less dangerous than fine comic art, especially that species Wilde raises to the level of genius. This is deeply troubling; for the truth is inescapable: in celebrating our folly, comedy is far more dangerous than tragedy.

The plot is fairly simple in outline: Sir Robert Chiltern, a politician of considerable prominence and skill is deemed by all to be a man of sterling character; he is idealized by his doting, admiring wife whom he loves deeply. A certain Mrs. Cheveley arrives on the scene of London's high society, and threatens to blackmail Sir Robert by means of a letter in her possession, which he wrote in his youth, that reveals serious misconduct during his earliest days in the government. She wants Sir Robert to persuade the government to support a doomed project concerning Argentine Canals, an act that would severely mislead investors. He is torn between his desire to retain his reputation and his duty as a member of the government to reject the Canal scheme. The pressure is exacerbated by his wife's insistence that she would never love a man whose moral character was not of the highest; so that exposure by Mrs. Cheveley of his letter would not only ruin his political career, but his marriage as well. Desperate for help and advice, Sir Robert turns to his life-long friend, the lover of trivial buttonholes, Lord Goring. Unexpectedly, the foppish charmer reveals deeper loyalty and devotion to decency than even that of Sir Robert's public image, resolving the crisis by a bit of blackmail of his own on the hapless Mrs. Cheveley, and incidentally winning the heart of Mabel Chiltern, Robert's sister. As a plot it is fantastical, following the banal development of a thousand lesser comedies; it is tangled with all the props of silly melodrama: people listening behind closed doors, compromising letters and notes falling into wrong hands, ridiculous exits and entrances causing embarrassments, mistaken identities, and the uncomfortable sense of Pollyanna when all turns out rosy. Yet, even on this banal level, there is a curious species of satisfaction: the triumph is not over blackmail, nor is it of good people over bad people, but of grace over scheming, even the scheming that outwits the blackmailer.

The danger that Shakespeare's poetry and Mozart's music may be mere autonomous reasons to appreciate their art requires us to see their beauty as fundamentally dramatic, and not merely an addendum to the comedic form. In Wilde's case, the danger is that the sparkling wit and delicious *bon mots* matter most, and the bawdy plot is but a vehicle for the delightful baubles. Wilde's wit, however, remarkable as it is, nevertheless yet serves the drama, rather than the other way around; so that it, too, is essential to his comedic art. The spirit behind these witticisms is a crucial *dramatic* element in the play, for taken too seriously they undermine morality, taken too lightly they beguile us into winking at their damage. Wilde both celebrates and censures this spirit, creating a palpable tension that persists far beyond the delight in the cleverness of the play. The battlefield for these opposing forces is found in the characters of the central figures.

Sir Robert's entrance in Act I is accompanied in the script by Wilde's description of him—a delight available only for readers, not the audience, which makes one wonder at the author's purpose. Did he love his readers more than his audience, or did he assume all who saw the play would want to buy the script, or was it simply beyond him to write anything that was not graced by cleverness? In any event, he says of Sir Robert that he is "A personality of mark. Not popular—few personalities are. But intensely admired by the few, and deeply respected by the many. . . . It would be inaccurate to call him picturesque. Picturesqueness cannot survive the House of Commons. But Van Dyke would have liked to have painted his head." This idol of moral rectitude is rather quickly revealed as one with a spotted past whose wealth and prestige were due to a criminal act of what today would be called insider trading. When approached by the wicked Mrs. Cheveley with the threat of blackmail, his puffing outrage is soon outclassed by the realization of the peril confronting him, and he agrees to support the Argentine Canal. However, when his wife assures him that his support would force her to leave him, he, and we the audience, realize the issue is far more grave than mere blackmail can resolve. Pressured by her, he is forced quickly to repudiate Mrs. Cheveley in a letter, and his doom seems inevitable. The scene deserves reflection.

As Mrs. Cheveley is about to leave the party at the Chiltern's house, she cattily informs Gertrude Chiltern that her husband now supports the Canal scheme. After the guests leave, Gertrude accosts her husband, pointing out that Mrs. Cheveley had been unscrupulous even when they had been schoolmates together. Robert says: "It is best forgotten. Mrs. Cheveley may have changed since then. No one should be entirely judged by their past." To which she responds: "One's past is what one is. It is the only way by which people should be judged." This Robert suggests, is "a hard saying," as indeed it is. Gertrude begins to reveal her true character: she is puritanic. Her remark allows for no redemption at all: once bad, always bad, denies the very essence of Christianity: forgiveness. Robert points out that circumstances may change, to which she replies "Circumstances should never alter principles. . . . It can never be necessary to do what is not honorable." She is entirely correct in this, of course; but following the hard and implacable position about the immutability of character, these fine sentiments sound merely harsh. When Robert appeals to "rational compromise," she says: "Robert, that is all very well for other men, for men who treat life simply as a sordid speculation; but not for you, Robert not for you. You are different. All your life you have stood apart from others. You have never let the world soil you. To the world, as to myself, you have been an ideal always. Oh, be that ideal still!" This seeming compliment is agonizing: Robert is being loved for his rectitude, not for himself. She then goes on: "Robert, is there in your life any secret dishonor or disgrace? Tell me, tell me at once, that—" Robert says: "That what?" to which she softly, slowly adds: "That our lives may drift apart." Here is true blackmail, far more sinister than the blackmail of either Mrs. Cheveley or, later, Arthur Goring. When Robert admits he would do anything rather than lose her, she forces him, immediately, to write a letter to Mrs. Cheveley telling her he will be resolute in rejecting the Canal scheme. This pressure is insidious: the mark of most puritanic blackmail is the hatred of reflection. Give the wavering sinner no chance to breathe or think, lest his shaky resolve be lost or a loophole be found. The pressure of speed and urgency has ever been the tool of enforced propriety of conduct, for it purloins judgment from the would-be sinner, leaving only the act good and not the agent. When Robert signs the fatal letter, Gertrude says: "I will love you always, because you will always be worthy of love." But if we are loved because we are worthy of it, not we, but our conduct is loved. More importantly, if we love only what demands our love, it is given out of duty, not grace. Gertrude, during the entire play save for the last redeeming moment, simply cannot love genuinely: she loves the ideal, not the husband.

Sir Robert, however, is not ideal at all. When he visits Arthur to bare his soul, he does not lament his crime in any way; he defends it. Arthur says, "I had no idea that you, of all the men in the world, could have been so weak . . ." Robert snarls: "Weak? Oh I am sick of hearing that phrase. . . . Do you really think, Arthur, that it is weakness that yields to temptation? I tell you that there are terrible temptations that it requires strength, strength and courage, to yield to. . . . to risk everything on one throw . . . there is no weakness in that. There is a horrible, a terrible courage in that." Robert is actually proud of his daring for that act of courage—and he is quite right in this insight: some unscrupulous acts take enormous courage, and consequently we should not refer to the agent as weak. Robert was not weak; he was corrupt; and even eighteen years later he still admires his own boldness for it provided him with the three things he cherishes most: money, power, and Gertrude. It is only after the dire catharsis of the plot that he realizes his love of Gertrude ranks above the other two. It is important to realize this almost Nietzschean view: Robert never, even at the play's end, rejects his crime. He is curiously too honest a man to deceive himself like that. What he rejects is Gertrude's indirect love for him as an ideal husband, which means he is not loved for himself. When his wife learns from Mrs. Cheveley that Robert's whole life of success began with dishonor, Gertrude shrinks in horror from him, saying: "You sold yourself for money. . . . You wake terrible memories—memories of things that made me love you—memories that are now horrible to me. And how I worshiped you. You were to me something apart from common life, a pure thing, noble, honest, without stain. The world seemed to me finer because you were in it. . . . And now—oh, when I think that I made of a man like you my ideal! the ideal of my life!" This cry of anguish from his wife allows Robert to say what is crucial to the entire dramatic point: "There was your mistake. There was your error. The error all women commit. Why can't you women love us faults and all? Why do you place us on monstrous pedestals? We have all feet of clay, women as well as men; but when we men love women, we love them knowing their weaknesses, their follies, their imperfections, love them all the more, it may be, for that reason. It is not the perfect but the imperfect, who have need of love. . . . All sins, except a sin against itself, Love should forgive." Lurking in this antipuritanic outrage is an indictment against Gertrude herself, for *she* is guilty of the one unforgivable sin, the sin against love itself.

Into this maelstrom of conflict enters Arthur Goring. It is not without irony that both Gertrude and Robert turn to this dandy for succor. If he is so "trivial," why do both seek him out? Gertrude tells him that Robert is "as incapable of doing a foolish thing as he is of doing a wrong thing," to which Arthur, after a long pause, remarks, "Nobody is incapable of doing a foolish thing. Nobody is incapable of doing a wrong thing." Gertrude then accuses him of being a pessimist. "No, Lady Chiltern, I am not a pessimist. Indeed I am not sure that I quite know what Pessimism really means. All I do know is that life cannot be understood without much charity, cannot be lived without much charity. It is love, and not German philosophy, that is the true explanation of this world, whatever may be the explanation of the next." This is a moving speech, but speeches do not constitute the essence of dramatic art, drama does; and it is in the dramatic unfolding that we see concretized what Arthur says in the speech.

The tableau is of the stuff of bawdy license; it is silly in itself; but it serves to unveil the tension in the character. In the third act, Arthur having received a dangerously worded note form Gertrude that she intends to visit him that evening, and distracted by his father's unforseen arrival, instructs his servant to escort the arriving lady into the drawing room; but the lady who appears is not Gertrude but Mrs. Cheveley, and the servant unwittingly installs her where Arthur expects and believes Gertrude to be hidden. Sir Robert unexpectedly arrives, putting Arthur in a highly anomalous and comic dilemma. When a chair is knocked over in the drawing room, Robert demands to be informed, and Arthur tries to restrain him. "Do you give me your word that there is no one there?" "Yes," Arthur says. "Your word of honor?" "Yes." Here is a moment challenging the director and actor. Is Arthur's second "yes," on his word of honor, to be given reluctantly or glibly? The word of a Victorian English gentleman, made on his honor, should matter even to a dandy. If the audience senses hesitation, we realize he is making a genuine sacrifice: but for Arthur the love for a friend outranks even one's word of honor. Or: if the lie is glibly told, we might feel that honor does not matter to the Arthurs of the world, and the lie simply shows us that Arthur is unscrupulous in his avoiding uncomfortable situations. Both readings are attractive, though I have a slight preference for the first, since it intensifies Arthur's character. Here is a man for whom loyalty to friends outranks honor; but paradoxically, since loyalty is itself honorable, perhaps he truly embodies honor more than the mere formalities of it; this is doubly so if the loyalty is grounded in loving friendship. Perhaps it is not loyalty but love that outranks honor. Whether he hesitates before giving his second "yes," we nevertheless recognize that the situational farce is not what makes this play comedic art: the deeply serious matter of character in the crucible of conflicting loyalties emerges. What Arthur *says* in the Second Act about love explaining who we are is here *shown*: Arthur will not let his status as a gentleman outrank his loving loyalty to his friend Robert, but Gertrude's wifely love does not reach that far into the footage of forgiving grace. The puritanic is horrified at Arthur's ranking; but even the nonpuritanic is uneasy; for the danger is that Arthur's choice may seem mere romanticism. We do not want words of honor to be discarded merely on some sentimental attachment to extracting ourselves form embarrassment. Does the play really go this deep? Why should the tension between Arthur's integrity as gentleman dandy and as friend matter that much? Is not the sheer folly of the situation sufficient to entertain us? If it were a farce, perhaps; but it is comedic art. These questions about the legitimacy of such "deep" reading are easily resolved when we turn to the denouement, where Wilde's genius cannot be avoided.

Consider the real problem that confronts us when we reflect on this comedy. It is not the paradox of outwitting a blackmailer by blackmail or the moral dubiety of keeping a once-corrupt politician in office. After Mrs. Cheveley slinks back to Austria, defeated, we are left with a far more troubling problem: understanding Gertrude's reversal. Just at the moment in the fourth act at which Robert is saved from blackmail, the prime minister offers him a cabinet post. Gertrude once again enters like a scolding harpie, persuading Robert to turn down the cabinet seat and return, chastened, to the dull but decent life of a country gentleman. She points out that Robert must reject the offer since the basis for it, his apparent integrity, is undeserved. Once more Gertrude presses him to write the letter of resignation immediately; she has learned nothing from the harrowing experience with Mrs. Cheveley; she is still puritanic in her remorseless urgency to do what she deems the right thing. Arthur again intervenes, and as a result she allows Robert to accept the post, after all. Then, in a wonderfully ironic twist, it is Robert, of all people, who becomes puritanic and pedantic, refusing to allow his sister Mabel to marry Arthur, the man to whom he owes his marriage and career! The reason given for this shocking ingratitude is that Robert had heard Arthur's praise of the woman hiding in the drawing room. Anyone who so dotes on Mrs. Cheveley cannot be worthy of his sister. Arthur, not wanting to expose Gertrude, nobly refuses to defend himself; but when Gertrude herself explain it was she, and not Mrs. Cheveley, who was supposed to be there, that final snarl is unsnarled and all is well. Or is it? How are we to understand Gertrude's remarkable *volte face*? Consistency of character is the one essential quality demanded of great playwrights, for without this consistency we are left solely to the techniques of ridiculous plots where the rankest serendipity both causes and resolves all problems. If character is to outrank plot in order for a mere farce to be turned to genuine comedic art, then it might seem that Wilde, in his need to resolve the comedy, has erred in having Gertrude act inconsistently with her true nature. How are we to understand her nonpuritanic grace that so graces the final scene with redemption? This question is of supreme importance if we are to unlock the true spirit of great comedy from its confines within a merely pleasant bedroom farce.

We must go back a bit to do this question justice. Mrs. Cheveley's blackmail of Robert, troubling and unscrupulous though it may be, nevertheless is based on truth; Robert was indeed guilty of a dishonorable act. Furthermore, in the harsh world of power politics, such low scheming is an acceptable, though still morally dubious, strategy. The woman does not act out of cruelty, but simply dire necessity; she needs the money, and this is the best way to get it. She is even willing to surrender the damning letter to Arthur if he agrees to marry her. In this atmosphere of low cunning, even Mrs. Cheveley is able to tell Gertrude that she, as blackmailer, pities Gertrude the puritan: she actually feels sorry for what Gertrude had become! And we, the audience, hearing this, cannot help but agree. Gertrude appears more wicked than Mrs. Cheveley. But the next step deserves note. Earlier in the play Arthur had discovered a curious piece of jewelry which he recognized as a brooch-bracelet he had originally given his cousin and which Mrs. Cheveley had stolen. After she admits it was hers, Arthur attaches it to her wrist, then threatens to call the police, for he now can prove she is a thief. Blackmailed by this threat, Mrs. Cheveley is impelled to give Arthur Robert's letter, which he then burns. As he does so, Mrs. Cheveley spots the pink stationary on which Gertrude had written the compromising note to Arthur. She purloins this note, and threatens to send it to Sir Robert unless Arthur lets her go. Later, she sends it anyway, trusting it will destroy their marriage. This act reveals an ugliness not hitherto suspected; its origin is sheer malice, something done solely on the basis of cruelty and revenge, for it has no practical value. She has lost all chance of supporting the Canal scheme as well as her instrument of political destruction; Gertrude's note has already served its purpose in extricating her from Arthur's threat to have her arrested; beyond that it has no purpose, yet she sends it to Robert solely as an act of hatred, to hurt Gertrude and to exalt in it. All possible sympathy for her is now lost; she no longer can legitimately feel sorry for Gertrude, for while blackmail may be less shameful than puritanism, outright cruelty is far worse than either.

This inevitable shift of sympathy from the blackmailer to the now-victim, Gertrude, is matched by a change in that lady herself. This puritan is now willing to lie, to cheat, to steal, to beguile, and to deceive, simply to get the innocently written but now dangerously compromising note back. She finds herself in her husband's shoes, not only circumstantially, but also morally. She, as he, wills dishonorable means to keep her honor. But furthermore, like Robert, Gertrude, in her cunning, now turns to Arthur to abet her impropriety. Always gracious rather than principled, Arthur readily agrees. In an irony that sparkles with genius, however, Robert has already received the letter, but reads it, not as a token of his wife's infidelity, but as plea from her to him! No deceit or theft is necessary. It could have stayed that way, an innocent misreading making all things right, until Robert turns on Arthur, refusing him Mabel's hand. Arthur is stunned; nevertheless out of loyalty to Gertrude, he says: "I have nothing more to say." This self-sacrifice moves Gertrude to admit she had written the note to Arthur—a dangerous move. But by this time the truth can be revealed, and even Robert can laugh at this joke on himself. This resolves the comic anguish but not the thinker's problem: how are we to understand Gertrude's sudden reversal? Several possibilities suggest themselves:

1) She herself was forced to rely on unprincipled acts to save her honor; perhaps this makes her more sympathetic to Robert's having done so. The trouble with this is that after such learning she still, puritanically, insists on Robert quitting politics.

2) She sees, with Arthur's prompting, that Robert's sacrifice is greater than hers, and realizing that sacrifice makes for the greater love, is eager now to offer her own sacrifice. This is a much more generous reading, and is probably true; but it follows from a conversion rather than explains a conversion.

3) It is far more practical. Arthur points out that such a move would eventually destroy their marriage, since it would cause Robert to resent her. She "converts" merely to save her marriage. This may also be partly true, but it, too, seems more a consequent than a cause. After all, she herself earlier threatened separation if Robert proved dishonorable; why should her marriage matter so much now when it did not matter so much then?

4) Her willingness to use dishonorable means to save her marriage reveals she really does love Robert more than she idealizes him. This certainly is true; but it leaves out why it took so long, and why she still insists he quit politics. Perhaps if we accept all four, their combined weight suffices.

Perhaps. A fifth possibility however may be suggested that satisfies on a far deeper level. Its truth is easily stated: the real victim of puritanism is the puritan. Gertrude at first thought she loved Robert for his nobility; it was her puritanism that blocked her from realizing she also loves him for himself. The irony that Robert becomes puritanic as Gertrude becomes less so, is irresistible. Arthur's keen insight into his friend is disturbing: he tells Gertrude Robert will, deprived of power, come to hate her as its cause. Gertrude earlier believed (falsely) that were Robert to be shown dishonorable they would have to part. But Gertrude does indeed learn he was dishonorable, and rather than separating, she plots, schemes, and endangers herself for his sake, proving to all except herself that she loves him, not his perfection. It was her puritanism that blinded her. Robert's magnificent passage about men loving women for their faults is proven backward, for if Arthur is right, it is Gertrude who, when pressed, makes the nobler sacrifice. Arthur's prediction about the eventual outcome of Robert's rejecting the post is cruelly knotted to his deep understanding of his friend's character: he is power-hungry and ambitious and even now still defends his youthful gamble, but Arthur still loves him as a friend. It is not merely that Gertrude realizes her marriage would collapse if Robert resigned the post, it is rather that, seen through the prism of Arthur's continued affection, she realizes that she too, loves him, even knowing his true, flawed character.

There is nothing wrong—indeed there is much splendidly glorious—about loving someone because they are good and noble. Gertrude still believes in many of her noble sentiments, because they are indeed true. The danger is not in loving someone who is good, but in leaving the "someone" out, loving only the good. But good unlinked to persons is not good at all. When Gertrude tears up Robert's letter of resignation she is not inconsistent with her character but only with what her puritanism had allowed her character to resemble. If we consider the whole play we realize that what Gertrude *says* about loving only nobility is throughout denied by what she *does*. It takes Arthur's persistence in his own friendship to awaken in her what she truly feels. We must consider what she now embraces: she will love Robert knowing he not only made a youthful error, but yet now still retains those characteristics that made him do it. Robert was willing to sacrifice his post for Gertrude; but Gertrude was willing to sacrifice much more: her idealism.

Arthur's persuasion of Gertrude not to insist that Robert quit politics deserves analysis. It is not primarily what he *says* that convinces her; rather it is his own character that, when revealed, shows Gertrude who she really is. Arthur reveals to her his own deep insight into Robert's flaws; but he also shows that despite those flaws, he continues to cherish him as his friend. Seeing the depth of that devotion and affection, Gertrude realizes that she, too, has similar depths, and having them she is enabled to do what she does. This is again the triumph of grace over mere duty. Once more it is possible for the reader of the script to gain insight denied the mere observer, for, as Arthur prepares himself to persuade Gertrude, Wilde offers this stage direction: "Pulling himself together with a great effort, and showing the philosopher that underlies the dandy . . ." For Wilde, it is Arthur as *philosopher* that proves his finest mettle. How does this mesh with Arthur's earlier remark that it is love and not German philosophy that shows us who we are? The answer is obvious: the term *philosopher* here is used in its original sense of loving truth. Arthur will lie glibly in social affairs and to save his friends, but such lying is not inimical to the reverence for truth; it is his philosophical truth as loyal friend more than the practical truth that Gertrude's pressure will destroy her marriage that persuades. This reading of the text seems to provide a more satisfying understanding of Lady Chiltern's unexpected grace; for it is based on reverence for truth.

If Gertrude's last-minute triumph over puritanism troubles until we discover its deeper meaning, a similar, though perhaps less important, unexpected reversal also deserves reflection. Throughout the entire play the comical character of Arthur's father, the Earl of Caversham, urges his bachelor son to marry; but this charming playboy not only dismisses his father's concerns, but makes countless deprecatory remarks about the unhealthy dangers of that institution. In the fourth act his sudden and unexpected proposal to Mabel seems out of character with this lover of triviality. How are we to understand *his* reversal? This puzzle is far easier to unravel than that about Gertrude; but it still deserves consideration. Mabel's own character is obviously part of the explanation. Of all the clever if attractively scandalous aesthetes, Mabel seems the most frivolous, yet the most cheerful. Even more than Arthur she seems irreverent of the serious, giggling away all pomp and pomposity, treating the proposals of poor Tommy Trafford with lighthearted contempt and disdain. When Arthur tells her he has something "very particular to say," she responds rapturously: "Oh, is it a proposal?" When Arthur is taken aback by this she says, "I am so glad. That makes the second today." Few responses in the entire arsenal of feminine guile are more crushing—she is delighted by the number! Yet for all her silliness she has remarkable integrity, linked to a high spirit of fun that defuses all her barbs; and in her own direct, honest way, she confesses immediately that she had been longing for his proposal for quite some time. We sense this will be a merry union, perhaps not unlike that of Beatrice and Benedick. But even granting the propriety of his choice, how do we account for the diehard bachelor suddenly offering to give up his independence? One account is that just as Arthur and eventually Gertrude love Robert in spite of his corruption, so he also embraces marriage knowing of its dangers. A second point is that he has just witnessed the power of the sacrament to lift two flawed participants, Robert and Gertrude, to levels of the highest sacrificial grace, because of that institution. A third is that of all human phenomena, why and with whom we fall in love is never to be explicated, but accepted. This third point may explain his love, but not his marriage. Perhaps knowing Mabel, the only way he could have her is by marrying her, and so he cedes his bachelor status simply to fulfill his longing. There is some truth is these three suggestions; and they may even suffice. A fourth suggestion, however, is not out of place.

Perhaps Arthur's proposal should be seen in light of the comedic art itself, in which a parallel is drawn between Gertrude and Arthur. Arthur's rejections of marriage may be due to his dandyism, just as Gertrude's failure to realize she loves Robert for himself and not merely his goodness is due to her puritanism. Dandyism masks the philosopher; Arthur pretends to be trivial precisely because he is deep. Both puritanism and dandyism deceive us by seeming to disenable true love; indeed, true dandyism and true puritanism would indeed render genuine love impossible. Just as we learn Gertrude is not merely or entirely puritanic so Arthur is revealed as not merely or entirely a dandy. In their extremes, both dandyism and puritanism are deeply antagonistic to both love and truth; it is the triumph of both love and truth over these two antagonists that makes the play high comic art. If this parallel of Arthur's reversal to Gertrude's is legitimate, the person who enables him to reveal himself, Mabel, becomes all the more significant. In contrasting Mabel to Mrs. Cheveley a deeper insight into Wilde's dramatic craft can be learned.

Both Mabel and Mrs. Cheveley participate in the prevailing vogue of London's high society, denouncing moral restraint by brilliant witticism and deliciously wicked *bon mots*. Wilde himself was a champion in this arena, but it was a fairly universal game played by many sophisticates. Churchill did it with no lack of brilliance, as did Mark Twain. In part, much of this playing can be seen as a reaction to the morally stifling atmosphere of the Victorian age, which had an unintended negative effect on morality by linking it to such unrealistic attitudes toward sexual conduct that a certain artificiality of deceit was almost imperative. Indeed during that period, "morality" almost became identified with sexual puritanism, so that "being wicked" was simply being lustful. Nevertheless, the prevailing wit bore with it a dangerous license: the proper thing was seen as pretending in public to be chaste, but privately winking at indiscretion; a practice that had ruinous effect on respect for both decency and truth. For Mrs. Cheveley, this atmosphere of winking at impropriety entailes justification of improper conduct. For Mabel, who is just as clever, such winking is comic, recognizing folly and weakness without condoning it. The atmosphere of deceit that lies behind such droll wit provides Mrs. Cheveley with a dangerous justification for profoundly immoral behavior; but Mabel sees in the same deceit not license, but the endorsement of human folly that is the loving essence of comic art. In the prior chapter, the discussion of Cherubino noted that though we must and do distinguish simple lust from erotic love, it is not always possible to spot the demarcation. The same can be said here: what is it that demarks comic embracing of folly from moral endorsement of being foolish? It is glib enough to write down they are different; it is genius to show us Mabel and Mrs. Cheveley. When Lord Caversham assures Mabel that his son Arthur should make her an ideal husband she says: "An ideal husband! Oh, I don't think I should like that." There is wisdom in this; it is, however, not a license allowing Arthur to be unfaithful. What she wants is not that he be an ideal husband but that she be a "true" wife. Those are her words, "true wife." Perhaps Arthur will be a true, if not an ideal, husband.

If this play reflects the essence of true comedy it is precisely because of the subtle but profound difference between the warm embrace of human folly and the endorsement of foolish behavior—the difference between Mabel and Mrs. Cheveley. If what enables the difference is the ineffable charity embodied in Arthur Goring, and latently discovered in Gertrude, the truth that emerges is worth the very real risk of sponsoring an indifference to morality. We can laugh with rather than at the antics of Arthur, Robert, Gertrude, and Mabel because, though they are foolish, their folly rests in part on genuine love that redeems, and their eventual triumph can be celebrated because their faults are the faults of lovers. Mrs. Cheveley can be laughed at; though at her final cruelty we do not laugh at all, but feel uneasy at the extent of her malice. It is the presence of what Arthur calls charity that gives the play its friendly, intimate sense of worth: without this grace the follies of the characters would at best present a pleasant distract; with it, truth-revealing art occurs; we are not merely entertained; rather, our own truth is illuminated, once we are rendered a new strength, which enables us to embrace this wondrous, if dangerous, truth.

V

Folly

REFLECTION on these three plays suggests that what is shared by them as an essential part of their success as art works is grace enabled by folly. Yet the three lovers, Silvius, Cherubino, and Arthur, anatomized by the comic scalpel, are entirely distinct. Cherubino's love-folly, being erotic, is the most dangerous; Arthur's, being Christian charity, is the most virtuous; Silvius's, being devotional, is the purest. These three stem from fundamentally different spirits; to designate them all as love reveals the vast reach of that embracing term. Yet it is their radical difference that ironically helps us understand the curious union of grace and folly that is the essence of comic art. Without this union the dramas would fall short of their excellence; with it they are paradigms. It is, however, neither folly nor grace that explain comedy, but comedy that explains folly and grace; we must first learn the dramas before we can learn their meaning—an approach that is antitheoretic, and hence somewhat out of favor in our present age. These great comedies will, and already have, outlasted their theories, and in outlasting them outclasses them as well. The diversity of the three species of loving requires a far deeper critique—that is, a truly philosophic critique—than any mere theoretical account can provide. This must be emphasized: graced folly is worthy because it uniquely reveals truth. It is truth discovered in no other way: without the loftiest comedies, we would lack a precious resource that is absolutely essential for understanding who we are. Folly without grace becomes the merely ridiculous, and can be laughed at jeeringly; grace without folly becomes a mere cheat on justice, at which we should weep, and not laugh at all.

If great comedy fuses folly and grace, it were both foolish and ungracious to analyze these terms independently, as if folly were one thing and grace another, and bringing them together were a mere occasional coupling, the way we occasionally couple nights with storms, for not all nights are stormy nor are all storms at night. Yet, though in comic truth grace is not truly grace without folly nor folly truly folly without grace, we must distinguish them, for they do not mean the same thing. Since we the audience are fools, we can perhaps begin with some concrete spade work on the hard soil of the new garden by asking: How are we to understand our three comic friends as fools? The fundamental insight seems to be that we laugh with them because their folly is based on love. But why should love make us foolish? And why should our witness of love-based folly have the remarkable effect on us that brings us back to the theatre over and over, and compels us to think so deeply on the matter? The danger to be resisted here is to interject theoretical accounts onto the phenomenon rather than letting the phenomenon reveal its secrets. When Silvius runs away from Corin crying, "Oh, Phebe, Phebe, Phebe!" (II,4) or Cherubino pleads for illumination on his burning and shivering; or Arthur imperils his chances to wed Mabel by saying, "I have no more to say," we feel the wrenching of countersentiments: all three are making fools of themselves; yet all three endear themselves to us because of this. What is the essence of this folly?

Whatever else it is, folly is a lack or a negation. In ordinary usage it may mean the mere absence of knowledge, as when we distinguish the wise from the foolish. Usually such ignorance is of the practical rather than the theoretical, as when Christians read the parable of the seven wise and the seven foolish virgins: the latter had not prepared themselves with sufficient oil to light their lamps throughout the night. In this sense, folly is seen as a moral fault—they ought to have known—with unhappy consequences. It is contrasted with prudence. Certainly Silvius, Cherubino, and Arthur imperil their happiness by acting imprudently, being addled by love. Yet, they are not unaware of this: they *know* they are imprudent, but risk the dangers anyway. This self-awareness has a double effect: it seems to indict them of even greater folly; yet it also makes us pause. Can folly be folly if it be recognized? Who is more foolish: the man who enters a field ignorant of the dangerous bull feeding there, or the man who enters knowing the bull is there? The latter is surely more foolish. For the first man, folly is mere ignorance; but for the second folly seems far more insidious. It is reckless; and the recklessness makes us wonder why he does it. The moment we recognize there may be a reason, however, the imputation of folly may fade or disappear. If he has a compelling reason—if we learn he is being chased by a murderous enemy—it may even be wise to take the lesser risk with the bull than face the more dire one intent on mayhem. Lovers, however, do not fit this scenario, for they do not weigh carefully one risk against another. Firstly, though they may realize their own folly, as Silvius certainly does since he tells us so, they yet still may be confused. Is folly then the mere confusion that is residual? Secondly, they seem to feel a compulsion to risky behavior in spite of their knowledge that there is a risk. Is folly, then, nothing else except this imprudence compelled by love? Is it compulsion or confusion, or both, that makes us foolish? Both compulsion and confusion are species of lacking: in the first we lack control, in the second we lack clarity. Cherubino laments his confusion, Silvius his compulsion; yet both boys suffer both states. Arthur does not lack control so much as he surrenders it; he allows Gertrude to tell the truth that will save him; he will not do it on his own. To be lacking in control or clarity is to be foolish, to be lacking in both is doubly foolish, and lovers seem to lack both.

Yet, though folly must be a lack, it cannot merely be negative. We usually do not attribute folly to everyone equally simply because we are all ignorant about some things, for then folly would be rendered meaningless as an indictment. We are neither entirely ignorant nor entirely enslaved, for if we were either we could not be indicted at all. Confusion is not total ignorance, for I must know enough to realize I am confused. Compulsion is not the same as obsession, else we could not hold the lover responsible. Folly, therefore, seems as much a species of control and knowledge as it is of compulsion and ignorance. When Cherubino pleads for enlightenment he is not entirely unaware that he is in love and that he knows it, yet his plea is not inauthentic for that reason. When Silvius protests he is "all service" he is not thereby removing his responsibility, yet his protest is genuine. The ignorance inherent in folly is therefore of a very special kind: it is an ignorance that is reflective, and hence entails a species of wisdom. The compulsion of folly is also of a special kind: it is an enslavement that enables us to be more gloriously free. These are paradoxes, to be sure, but they are not unthinkable or logically incoherent. Reflective ignorance and liberating enslavement seem contradictions only in schemes of exceptionless and implacable laws, the way any reductionist metaphysics would explain the world; such a scheme inevitably leaves out persons, even or especially those persons who speculatively impose the schemes. As long as there are persons, especially persons that are comic audiences, reflective ignorance and free bondage must be able to be thought.

Yet, it is not these existential possibilities that make comedy possible; rather, it is comedy that enables these existential possibilities.

If folly is, at least in two species of its meaning, reflected ignorance and free bondage, we must submit to the need to seek further into what this means; and the strategy that emerges is that the most obvious, ironically, is the most mysterious. The first truth that is irresistibly obvious is that a fool cannot be entirely ignorant; but *not* being entirely ignorant is then the mystery: how can the non-ignorant be a fool? What does the fool know, and of what is he ignorant? What he knows and does not know is the same thing: his own folly. Lovers know they love; they also are confused by their ignorance; they seem addled by their own reality; the more they learn the depth of love, the more confused they become. Yet lovers are curiously unwilling to surrender this agonizing state. As Orlando says: "I would not be cured, youth." Somehow their cognizance of their own confusion is proudly borne, not unlike the soldier proudly showing his wound as the red badge of courage.

Yet, it seems we call a comic lover a fool not only because he manifests a glorious confusion, but also because he is led by this to do ridiculous and even dangerous acts. It is foolishly imprudent for Cherubino to undress in the Countess's bedroom and equally imprudent, but even more foolish, for the Countess to let him be there. This folly as imprudence cannot be endorsed morally for the risks are grave indeed. Yet surely this caveat is itself puritanic: should comedies tell us only stories in which lovers take merely moderate risks? This jolts. Lovers are not moderate anyway, and the gravity of the risks is muted greatly by aesthetic distance. It would not be a comedy if the Count's jealousy were to result in Cherubino's death; it would not be a tragedy either—it would simply be a hideous mistake and as a play no one would want to see it performed. The point, of course, is not the risk as risk but the risk as folly. Imprudence is a vice; but watching the imprudent manifestating folly scarper off with impunity, especially if the escape seems so unlikely that it is not taken seriously, removes the moral censure, allowing the folly to be appreciated for its own sake. Thus, we see that the utter silliness of most comic plots plays an unexpectedly profound role: if extrication from dire situations is accomplished by the wildest serendipity of fortune, the emphasis is shifted from the plot's probability to the more earnest matter of the character's folly. If this character's folly is based on feeble-mindedness, the success is minuscule; but if it is based on love-folly, it is majestic. The comic hero does indeed take imprudent, and thus morally dubious or even outright immoral, risks. This imprudence, as immoral, is a genuine part of human folly. But when the imprudence is defanged by unlikely spasms of serendipity, and presented with the safety of aesthetic distance, the folly is denuded of its moral censure, and can be seen as a resource for truth.

The imprudence of folly need not always be dire; and in the hands of genius the very insignificance of the imprudence produces a similar isolation. The plot of *As You Like It* relies less on the serendipity of coincidence than any other major comedy; the drama unfolds due almost entirely to the calculated projects of thoughtful characters. Once the scene shifts to Arden, the consequences of love-folly are not dire at all. Orlando's folly does not imperil in any way: his "imprudence" is to garland the forest with silly poems that rhyme Rosalind's name with a comic strain on both homophony and meter. Rosalind's disguise is prudent; she believes she is safer accoutered as a boy. Even Silvius's dotage is not imprudent, except as a provocation to his own misery. This is gentle folly, and hence only mildly imprudent. Yet, the calculated cunning of Rosalind reveals the true folly of the lovers by making them seem to be without hope, which is why Silvius is so pivotal. It is supremely foolish to love without hope. That only Rosalind knows there is hope intensifies the poignancy of this; and the audience, knowing of her planning, can witness joyfully the aching hopelessness of Silvius and Orlando just because their despair will soon be translated to joy. Imprudence is the immoral part of being foolish; comedy removes the consequences of the imprudent, leaving folly bereft of its censure. This cheats on the moral, but in cheating, it reveals a truth otherwise unreached.

These reflections are easily trivialized if we fail to ask a more revealing question: is the love that motivates these three comic fools endorsed in spite of their folly or because of it? To elect the former is to say that the comic strategy links love with folly precisely to show that even among fools love is redemptive. This is a powerful suggestion, for it shows that love is not eclipsed by imprudence. It is akin to the almost sacred regard we have for the safeguards of justice, insisting that even if some felons go free it is still better to require that the burden of proof is on the prosecutor, and that all, no matter how unsavory, must be presumed innocent. By ranking the reverence for presumed innocence beyond the concern for punishing all who deserve it, the true significance of a free society is celebrated. If even the wicked are protected by our rules, these rules take on a semi-sacred status. If even fools can be loved, the power of love's redemption is intensified by including even those who are imprudent and unwise. The allure that this suggestion has cannot be dismissed, for it is effective and may even help ease some of the paradoxic in comic art. It is lethal for the truth, however. We do not embrace the comic lover in spite of his folly but because of it; indeed perhaps he could not even be a lover at all without also being a fool. Wilde's play most clearly emphasizes this: Mabel does not want an ideal husband, but a human one—perhaps even a gloriously foolish one.

It is not enough, then, to note that in comedy the lovers are fools; it is rather that their foolishness reveals them as both lovers and beloved. Not all folly is comic, and thus not love-linked. But can we say that all love-based folly is comic and hence redemptive? This is a much harder question, because to deny it seems to unravel all authority in what has been suggested thus far. If we deny that all or any love-based folly is comic, then we must say that only *comically* love-based folly is comic, and the entire argument is then reduced to the hissing smoke of circularity with all the fire of validity doused by the water of critique. Yet, it seems implacably obvious that not all love-based folly is comic, for in the throes of an erotic love we may easily imperil ourselves by an imprudence that is lethal, unsavory, immoral, or all three. Because of this truth it seems we must return to the awful threat that only comically love-based folly is comic. What is needed is to realize that this circularity is not a fallacy; and this is accomplished by the realization that the term *comic* has slightly different meanings; a refinement that saves us from the ignominy of circularity. We then can alter the claim slightly and say that only comically love-based folly is comedic; thereby spotting the adverb as a species of art, and the adjective as that which distinguishes one kind of folly from another. Thus, the sentence can be read: only artfully presented (in comedies) loved-based folly is warmly (comically) endorsed as truth-revealing of our human frailty. This maneuver may seem a mere internal, philosophical game, playing with idle tactics, avoiding circularity by redefinition, until we realize that this "solution" achieves a new focus. The true center of comedic art—or any performative art for that matter—is not on the stage but in the audience.

In a later chapter further reflection will be spent on the realization that the origins of comedy in a religious festival still linger, and thus we are not mere observers of finely presented stories unfolding on the stage, but actual worshipers participating in the sacred rite. It suffices now merely to realize that, as partakers of the ritual celebration the question can now be asked: what does it mean to be fools baptized into the ritual of comic spirituality? The last seven words can be provisionally bracketed: what does it mean to be a fool? To put the question this way enables comic truth to be more deeply confronted.

To be a fool is to be human: perhaps it is even more fundamental: it is to be a person. We are finite, and folly is that species of finitude that, being unshunnable, demands self-confrontation. Because we confront ourselves finitely, we must remain always something of a mystery to ourselves, but never to the point of total ignorance or total confusion. What man cannot understand he either kills or worships. Modern man does neither since he understands everything. When what is beyond our comprehension is ourselves, to kill what is incomprehensible in us is not suicide, but self-deception; this slaughter of the mystery within us is pre-comic, or at least anti-comic; perhaps it is prior to all art, but in any event, as self-deceptive, it is evil. Once we realize the darkness inherent in such self-slaughter of the mystery within us by self-deception, the need to worship provoked by art replaces the need to destroy, and this enables the wisdom of confronting our own mystery as mystery—in ritual. Since this confrontation with our finitude is itself finite, it pulls us back from ourselves to enable our seeing it, and this pulls us toward ourselves by reason of the truth learned by such seeing. To be pulled back and forward in this way is folly; to confront folly as folly is comic. Only comedic art, conceived as a species of worship, reveals this truth.

What it means to be a fool includes our own confusion at being finite persons. Yet to be a fool cannot be simply endorsed, as if recognizing our weaknesses somehow were to render us irresponsible and our imprudence endured with impunity. Folly in the moral world is unacceptable; we cannot escape censure merely because as finite persons we share a common frailty. Yet, being foolish is not the same as being wicked or evil, nor does it always entail acting immorally, or even performing acts that are wrong. Rather, folly requires a sense of being seen; in this sense it is more akin to that which enables shame rather than guilt. To *be* a fool is to be *seen* as a fool. The subtlety of this powerful truth cannot be allowed to distract us from the need to reflect deeply on its meaning. The suggestion can be put in bolder terms: to be a fool is to appear a fool. It is not so much that Silvius dotes on Phebe but that in doing so he presents himself to the sylvan populace, including himself, as foolish. To be spotted as a fool is a species of exposure in which the instinct is to cover up, not unlike that instinct to cover ourselves when publically denuded. Without this exposure, folly is impossible, for without it we are merely imprudent. Especially among the arrogant and the sensitive, being exposed in the modality of folly is acutely painful, perhaps even the greatest ill to be endured. The hapless Russian in Dostoyevski's story is here revealed in its deeper significance, for were the cart to be mired with no one to see it, the man would simply recognize the mere problem, and assess how best to remedy it. The one thing he would never do, if unseen, would be to kill his valuable horse. Why, then, does he destroy what is precious simply because he is seen? His plight need not be in itself foolish or imprudent; he renders it foolish by the shame of being recognized as a fool, and so recognized he becomes one. Shame is not guilt, the latter is moral, the formal is existential. For the guilty, atonement and restitution are the resources for the decent; escape from punishment or self-denial by means of self-deceit is the resource of the irresponsible. But for the shamed, the sole resource is to vanish, disappear, or at least to hide and cover. In the same way, mere imprudence can be atoned or corrected, but folly abuses our existential worth, making us seek the covering of darkness or distraction.

In the comic art, however, the exposure as a fool does not shame. Silvius himself, proudly, proclaims his folly, just as Orlando, proudly, proclaims his "illness" of being in love. When Puck observes the antics of the beguiled lovers he tells us, the audience: what fools these mortals be. We, being mortals, recognize the indictment: we are fools, else we would not be in the audience feeling strangely elated at being called fools. When the root of folly is love, we can affirm it. This does not mean that all comic characters are lovers—the Dogberry constabulary are not lovers—but that the play in which their antics are foolish must bear with it an atmosphere of love-folly. Indeed, the resentment of being made a fool still occurs in love comedies, often as a contrast. We note, for example, the bitter and unforgiving hatred shown by Malvolio when he is mocked. He is quite justified in his outrage, for he has been mightily abused; the audience is somewhat uncomfortable about his plight, as is his mistress Olivia, but nothing proves the autonomy of comedy more than that we do not allow our nascent moral sentiment for him to outrank our dismissal of his silliness. The reason is abundant: his hatred is entirely unforgiving. In this he should be compared with another victim of ungracious but unintented insult in the play, the seeming minor character of Antonio, the sea captain who loves Sebastian. He, too, is abused, but being confronted with the confusion, and being a lover, forgives. Malvolio, being arrogant beyond the point at which he can laugh at himself, writhes not so much for his personal discomfort in the prison, as for being publically shamed. His folly is exposed for all to see: at the root of his hatred and revenge is an unendurable shame. His feckless ire is thus laughed at rather than with.

Even when our folly is not seen by others, it is our own witness of this exposure to ourselves, rather than the mere moral responsibility we accept, that provokes shame. What, then, allows us to become the object of such exposure, and rather than shrink into eclipse, accept our folly as the origin of mirth, and pride in the spectacle of it? It is tempting to fill in the blank here with ready theories. Perhaps what allows us to reveal our folly shamelessly is that such folly is a universal condition of our humanity. Perhaps it is because it is based in love, and love is shameless. Perhaps it is because it is on the stage, and not in real life. Perhaps because as art, it is presented as beautiful, not as moral. Perhaps it just happens; or perhaps it happens for a reason that is best left undiscovered, for in discovering the reason we would destroy the art. Perhaps it is because it is happening to others and not ourselves. Perhaps it is because of grace, or truth, or forgiveness. There may be some validity in most of these suggestions, and taking them all together may satisfy. What yet must be learned, however, is the deeper paradox inherent in the realization that folly *shown* is distinct from mere foolish behavior—imprudence—or even from the general characteristic shared by all the human populace of being less than all-wise; and that this showing, though normally a source of shame, somehow becomes the basis for celebration.

To display oneself a fool is not the same as being made a fool *of*. Lear is made a fool of by his daughters; Iago makes a fool of Othello. The clever telemarketer makes a fool of the aged and infirm, and politicians commonly make fools of the electorate. In such cases cunning or cleverness outwits the more deserving, and the subsequent feeling of being mocked by the foxy tactics of the unworthy causes in the victims a great reluctance to be even further exposed in their vulnerability. In such cases, to speak of making a fool of the beguiled means to mock them either as so naive they feel disarmed and hence unwilling to take redress, or so gullible as to provoke glee in showing superiority over them, ranking the keen above the dull, the critical above the trusting. If we are made fools *of* by having our trust abused by cunning, perhaps the ability to celebrate our folly lies somehow in trust triumphing over mockery. This suggestion demands reflection on trust as a crucial element in comedic folly. Trust is not trust if certain: we do not trust the sun to rise, but are assured of it; to trust is to risk; the greater the risk the greater the trust. To trust the once untrustworthy is to gamble on what we deem to be hidden resources of integrity; to be shown that the risk was ill-advised is inherent in the risk. The difference then, between being revealed as a fool and being made a fool of is in part the difference between gullibility or naivete and trust; the latter can be legitimate even if consequentially hurtful, the former, never. What enables us to celebrate being shown a fool is the triumph of trust over certainty, and to discriminate one's own folly as trusting rather than naive. We can find mirth in our own being exposed as fools only if trust in our original worth cannot be eclipsed by the consequences of imprudence, particularly when that imprudence results from trust.

Trust is a virtue. It is a virtue inherent in being able to be fooled, hence is a virtue by dint of our humanity. It shares a great deal with another virtue that is possible only because of our flaws: courage. We cannot be courageous without fear any more than we can trust without risk. Those who fear fearing would have a world in which fear is impossible, but in such a world there would be no courage. To have a world where risk is impossible is to deny trust, and lacking trust, there would, in such a world, be no folly. But if courage can be gloriously celebrated, so can trust. If trust as trust risks, then to celebrate trust is to rejoice in folly.

The analogue, perhaps even overlap, to courage deserves further reflection. It is sometimes falsely assumed that courage is merely an extrinsic necessity for the accomplishment of higher virtues, such as justice or piety. We train young men to be warriors by instilling in them a sense of self-sacrifice that enables them to face huge dangers bravely. We do this, we say, in order to protect our society, our way of life. If there were no threat to what is ours, there would be no need of such training, and hence no need of courage. After all, courage is the one virtue it would seem we do not want to have: for courage requires fearsome conflict and agonizing self-doubt as to one's capacity to suffer, which are both singularly unpleasant. If we could have justice and wisdom and success without having to confront such pain, surely we would prefer it to the high cost of the precious currency, courage. Yet, even as we consider this, a certain unease accompanies the suggestion. Perhaps even were justice available without cost we might still rank the intrinsic worth of courage. We do not, for example, deem the young warrior on the losing side, dying of his sacrificial wounds, to be bereft of courage; indeed the very unsuccess of his offering may fill us with greater awe and wonder than that bestowed by the victor. Furthermore, it is patently inescapable that the manifestation of courage can be beautiful. We thrill to the vision of the young embracing risk, the old struggling to unburden their family of the huge cost of lingering death, or the educator sacrificing his own success to allow the student's wisdom to shine forth on its own. If courage is neither dependent on success nor lacking in beauty, perhaps we can and should say it has intrinsic rather than merely extrinsic worth. The same must be said for the trust that is of the essence of folly as a spectacle. It is simply worthwhile to be trusting, even if that trust can be abused.

Refinement of these suggested distinctions has now become imperative. Naive folly, even though it is less noble than that based on trust, can and does belong in the comic art. Even gullible folly, though far more discomforting and unworthy, can find occasional foothold in the masterful dramas, but less frequently, since the gullible are more pathetic than the naive. We can laugh warmly and fondly at the naivete of Peter Quince's goofy thespians in their assessment of what is proper for a courtly performance. Yet there is a deeper sense of appreciation for the trusting folly shown by Bottom's acceptance of Titania's wooing, his remarkable gentility in welcoming the playful spirits, Cobweb, Mustardseed, and Peasblossom, and above all his eagerness to have his own folly exposed by Peter Quince writing a ballad about his dream. It is therefore false to maintain that only trusting folly, and not naive folly, belongs in comedy. What helps tremendously in our understanding is to note the difference in a single play, and to realize the richer dimensions of folly grounded in trust. A play in which only the bawdy folly of naivete or even the wincing folly of the gullible, were present would succeed less than one containing trustful folly. That there can be such a thing as trust-grounded folly helps us to understand why we can accept the other forms of folly.

It is still true that imprudence in the practical world is a vice: it must be censored. But if imprudence is a vice and trust is a virtue, but trusting can be imprudent, are we not in danger of inconsistency? Trust is not the same as gullibility or naivete, yet what distinguishes them is not the painful consequence of imprudence since all three can have this; it is rather that trust, like courage, has intrinsic worth. The success of trust can gratify both in art and in life: the French Underground trusted in the Allies' promise to invade, and they were gratified when they learned the trust was not undeserved; the American armies on Bataan and Corregidor trusted General Marshall to send relief; they were bitter with justifiable resentment when they were left alone to surrender. Yet, their trust was part of their glory in the annals of war. Pamina trusts Tamino in the *Magic Flute*, and their mutual triumph is a joy to see. Yet comedy can also show us trust denied, or mocked. Two curious comedies deserve a brief visit in this regard. *Cosí fan tutti* is troubling, because the test put by the trusting suitors to their fiancés, backfires; the women do yield to the lovers switched in disguise, and Mozart's genius leaves us unsure which pairing is ultimately triumphant. To a lesser extent, the young lovers in *Midsummer Night's Dream* also seem inconstant, even granting the dissembling wrought by the magic flower's juice. Had Oberon not removed the spell, would Lysander have married Helena? And even when the spell is removed we wonder what this tells us. Shakespeare seems almost to be mocking romantic love itself. Does it matter whom we love? Or is it more important, or more silly, that we love at all? Is love under the influence of magic any less real than that under the spell of "true" love?—or is all love magic, so that the flower's juice is really unnecessary? How are we to think of Demitrius's switching his love back and forth with ease? Trust, within these two comedies, is both abused and amused; it fails and succeeds. We must not confuse love with trust; rather, we fuse trust and folly. Does this mean all trusting, or only unsuccessful trusting, is foolish? Surely the latter cannot be right; for trust must, like love, be blind. To say the gullible and the naive are not the same as the trustful may offer some solace to the thinker, but how can the riddled lover know which is which? This dilemma is less threatening than it might seem. We, the audience, can distinguish Bottom's naivete about courtly life from his trust in the worth of his dream; but even the lovers on the stage are not entirely beguiled by the difference. Silvius is not naively convinced Phebe will ever love him; he knows she may not; his glory is that he loves her anyway. His is a species of trust grounded in love, and hence is a species of folly, but it is not naivete. Consider Don José for a moment: Carmen tells him her love for him will be fierce but brief; he knows this, yet he loves her anyway, forever. We cannot call this naivete nor gullibility. He is, then, foolish to the point of silliness in his trust. What makes his a tragic rather than a comic folly is not that he loves without hope but that his love becomes obsession, and the audience senses the inevitability of fate rather than the serendipity of fortuity. One might also point out that Don José is well aware of Carmen's inconstancy, whereas Silvius is not entirely without hope; but these refinements tangle rather than clarify. There is no doubt that the plots of comedy and tragedy are often woven of the same strands of folly in our natures; we also note that sheer fortuity often keeps the comedy from being a tragedy; but the difference in the spirit of the two forms is vast. Both arts may be Dionysian, and Shakespeare proves one artist can succeed in both, but too much can be said about this linkage. The essence of comedy is folly, that of tragedy is fate. The use of Don José is simply to show that a dramatic character can be foolish without being naive or gullible.

There is, however, another difference that may be made to help us here. Naivete is not quite the same as innocence, and in comedy it is sometimes important to recognize the import of this distinction. The very youth of some comic lovers is often a redeeming quality of the very folly that endears. Cherubino is more innocent than naive. Consider that the original soprano who sang the role of Barbarina was, according to some musical historians, only twelve years old! If this is true, the youthful innocence of the love-trysts would have been an irresistible factor for the original audience. There is a sweetness about such innocence that softens our censure; the sheer novelty of experiencing love so freshly makes it a precious folly rather than a dangerous one. Cherubino is sung by a soprano, not a tenor; he is more boy than man. His trust stems from his youth, and though it still be folly and hence imprudent, the innocence of it endorses our acceptance of it. Beatrice and Benedick are not that young, and hence theirs is a different spirit of comedy altogether; Falstaff has long since abandoned all memory of innocence, so his folly is even more distinct. But in those plays where extreme youth provides the glow of innocence, the folly becomes all the more radiant. Naivete and gullibility among older characters are more obviously faults, and the inherent imprudence is thus more morally significant. It is not quite accurate, then, to call Cherubino gullible or naive; his is the folly of innocence. The music tells us so.

All these rather subtle distinctions are not meant to provide an algorithmic system of labels allowing us to resolve the paradox by putting characters in the right box. They are rather indications of the rich tapestry woven by comedic genius to present folly as a source of truth and celebration. The distinction between innocence and naivete is not as powerful or as important as the realization that comic folly must be denuded, and that such denuding is without shame. The difference between being shown a fool and being made a fool of is not the same as the foolish/silly distinction. Nor should we expect any reductionist answer to why love-folly is shameless; no mere taxonomy of psychological states can ever be produced to account for this. Rather, these reflections on the breadth and wealth of folly are meant to show what it means to be foolish and to recognize it in an art form. The insight that folly endorsed must be folly manifested is therefore of capital import in seeking to understand the genius of comedy. Were Silvius and Cherubino reluctant to expose their folly and even celebrate it in spite of the hurt or danger inherent in it, comedy, at least in its highest and noblest form, would not be possible. To watch fools glory in their folly delights us all the more since folly normally is a source of shame. What enables this shameless glory in folly is the denuding of love, especially erotic love.

Even with these distinctions that help us appreciate the rich complexity of what it means to be foolish, however, the earlier caveat needs reiteration. Folly by itself, even when it conforms to the two necessary conditions for comedy—that it be shamelessly revealed by the fool and that it be centered in the phenomenon of love—cannot suffice. Folly unlinked to grace is a quagmire: in its vast bog, widened now by our reflections to the size of a lake, we can only sink in confusion. The distinctions offered here when unlinked to grace prove more mettlesome and entangling than ultimately illuminating. It is necessary perforce to consider folly first and unlinked; that what we learn is from comedic folly and hence linked to grace can no longer be avoided. Grace unlinked to folly is also ultimately insufficient; but the needs of inquiry require it as a provisional step.

VI

GRACE

IT is glib enough to describe formally: grace is that species of worth or bestowal that is neither earned nor compelled, and is based rather on who we are than on what we do. It does not take a thinker long, however, to discover that this formal account is deeply disturbing in many ways, not the least of which is the dubiety concerning the distinction between doing and being, for what we do can and does alter who we are, and who we are often accounts for what we do. More serious is the apparent outrage against fairness and morality that seems inherent in the distinction, for if mercy or pardon is a species of grace, then justice is cheated and the authority of law is undermined. Yet, even if these problems are somehow overcome, a less obvious but even more perilous thwart to reason itself lurks behind not just the formal account but in the shadows of its real phenomena; this may provisionally be called the "paradox" of grace, though at this stage such appellation seems more sanguine than accurate. The paradox is that grace by its nature and definition favors, and what is favored is special or even unique, hence lacking in universality. What lacks universality cannot be used as a reason, nor argued for, nor analyzed critically; it has no philosophically explanative power, since it lacks authority and principle. To appeal to grace to explain something thus seems akin to the appeal to such imponderables as coincidence, luck, and fortune, which have no explanative power either.

With such formidable barriers, the task of making grace thinkable seems daunting, if not impossible.

To exacerbate the knottiness of this snarl I suggest that *only* comedic genius provides us with the wisdom or insight to confront this paradox. Without great comedy we would be unable to think philosophically about the meaning of grace. This would not mean that, bereft of comedy, there would be no gracious acts; it would mean that grace would be consigned to the same dubious pigeonhole of what Kant calls "usurpatory concepts"; that is, notions that appear to be explanative but really are not, such as luck and coincidence. It may even suggest something worse: that without the wisdom provided by the comedic art, grace would be a species of superstition, like believing in magical fairies, unworthy of a thoughtful mind. To claim that grace is a species of superstition is to claim that what we call grace is actually something else, usually something less lofty; a gracious act would then be reducible to a selfish act or to a disguised moral phenomenon. The superstition would be in the assumption that grace has any autonomy. Since we do indeed have and enjoy great comedy, this hideous suggestion need not be irresistible; indeed, few believe grace is superstition. It remains paradoxical, however; and only by accepting its paradox can we learn the great truth it has to offer. If the sole resource for confronting the paradox can be found in the philosophical reflection of comedy, it may then seem methodologically prudent to focus directly on the comic art; but since the issue here is the very paradox of grace itself, two general remarks refining the formal description may be helpful, followed by an analysis of what I shall call the four manifestations of grace. Only then can we turn directly to the illumination offered by comedy.

The first refinement of the formal account is that not all unearned benefits are gracious. Whether there be natural rights there certainly are institutional ones, such as those protected by our federal Constitution. Yet, though rights, natural or institutional, are certainly not earned since I inherited them at birth, it is obvious such rights are not the product of grace since *as* rights I have the right to them. It might be argued that the Constitution itself is a bestowal, and that may be true, which then would evoke in me a certain gratitude. But the right to freedom of expression or a trial by jury cannot be conceived as a gift and a right at the same time and in the same way, for rights can be demanded and gifts cannot. Thus to speak of gifts as unearned is insufficient. Unlike a right, a gift particularizes; its point is to single one person out as favored. Without this special sense of favoring, there could be no such thing as a gift at all, since if all bestowals are rights they are shared by all, and all would have an equal right to any gift, which would make it not a gift. We have done nothing at all to merit or earn the right to a jury trial; we say it is ours by right of being in America. It therefore is not by grace but by right. We have likewise done nothing to merit or earn a gift; but a gift is not a right hence it is the result of grace. How are we to understand this difference? As a mere refinement to the formal description it suffices to say that the difference just is the favoring of a specific person or persons; the nature and meaning of this favoring must be considered independently.

The second refinement concerns the ambivalence in the phrase *who we are*. This can mean at least two things: 1) who I am, particularly, and no one else, or 2) who I am as a person, shared by all persons. The point can be clarified concretely: I forgive you because you are my son; I would forgive no one else. Or: I forgive you because you are a person, and being a person you are unique, thus that uniqueness deserves some recognition which is provided by this act of forgiveness. As in the first, this refinement provokes the need for greater thought. We seem to be in the ridiculous position of saying: "We are all special." Of course, if we are all special then being special is shared by everyone and hence in being alike we are *not* special. The cowboy, Will Rogers, once said he never met a man he didn't like. Being liked by Will Rogers would then not mean very much, since he likes us all. In spite of this silliness, the Rogers quote seems to be saying *something*. There is a further refinement needed on this phrase. When we say "who we are" do we mean institutional identity, such as being this man's son, this woman's child? Or do we mean that we possess certain qualities and characteristics that make up our existential uniqueness independent of any familial or social relationship? Or do we mean simply that we exist as unique? Once again, the "refinement" seems to open up more problems than answers. By recognizing what these problems are, however, we have in fact already "refined" the formal account.

What I call the four manifestations of grace can be identified in the following ways: 1) forgiveness, 2) sacrifice, 3) favor, and 4) delight; the first two seem negative in some sense, the last two seem positive; but all four are troubling. A sketch of the problematic of each will be offered before turning to what is revealed about them by comedy.

FORGIVENESS. Forgiveness—which is here used in its broadest sense to include pardon and mercy—is often seen as a species or manifestation of grace; but when wanton or arbitrary it can be truly evil. It is harder to argue why it is not always evil. Doting parents who are profligate in their forgiveness of wayward children corrupt them by eroding all sense of responsibility; they also corrupt themselves by the self-deceit of deeming mere mawkish sentimentality as love. Good parents wisely both reward and bestow, making it clear which is which, so that the child takes satisfaction in receiving the promised wage for mowing the lawn, yet glows with warmth at the unexpected gift given simply because he is loved. The same fortunate child also knows when his punishment is deserved and given, and when it is deserved but pardoned. He is cheated even of the gift if he does not know he has earned the wage, for without merit to distinguish them, all bestowals come as rights, and neither gratitude nor accomplishment is possible. These commonsense reflections on pedagogy are troubling, however. Fairly strict parents may instill into their children a benign sense of the difference between merit and grace; lascivious parents may cheat their offspring of such keen appreciation, thereby denying them both; yet it is possible to say the stricter parents have a truer and deeper love than the overly generous or doting ones. It is also possible, however, to say the stricter parents are simply the more dutiful ones; they are doing what they ought to do. If we say the former, the entire education seems an existential bestowal; if the latter, it seems a moral demand. Does this reflection therefore undermine the very distinction between merit and grace?

It may be one of the most difficult judgments we can make. How far should the gracious encroach upon the moral? If I forgive every transgression I abet the wrong; if I do not forgive at all, the moral becomes oppression. When, and how often, should we forgive? The scriptural injunction of seventy times seven times does not mean that the four-hundred-ninety-first time is doom: it rather suggests: much more than you think, but not infinitely. The very word *should* exposes the fallacy of the question: if I should, or ought to, bestow, then I cannot bestow at all, since bestowal can never be required. The quality of mercy, Portia assures us, is not strained—meaning that it need not be given. But if bestowal has no "ought" or "should," it seems entirely unjustified. We know, though, that grace is a virtue. To say we cannot use rules, principles, algorithms, or paradigms to decide when to forgive, and hence forgiving is a judgment rather than an application, may seem to entail the arbitrary, suggesting that adherence to morality or justice is "objective," though with exceptions; whereas forgiveness is "subjective." Judgment, however, is never entirely subjective; it may be the link between subject and object. Even though we recognize this, the dark threat of arbitrariness and the misuse of "subjective" shows how serious the problem is. It is not only a problem for parents concerned with raising responsible yet existentially worthy children, it is a problem for the thinker: how do we understand grace if it threatens morality?

The traditional view sets the problem up in precisely this way. What is unquestioned is the moral; the questionable is the gracious. This seems the proper approach, for if justice requires punishment, as it sometimes does, then we must ask: what are the grounds for exceptions—that is: under what conditions can pardon be allowed? This approach seeks to find a moral justification for what seems essentially counter-moral; and the response is often given in terms of a broader and more flexible notion of morality. We might argue that occasional pardons actually produce greater reverence for law, for example; or we might confuse pardons with excuses, saying that children especially are only partly responsible given their innocence; or that pardon allows for the criminal to grow into a worthy citizen, the sinner to achieve redemption, the brat to learn beautiful manners; thereby changing true forgiveness into a species of moral or social engineering. Many of these traditional attempts actually render some pardoning into moral requirements rather than moral exceptions; but in any event the justification—which is itself a moral term—is always moral.

Comedy, when properly thought and truly enjoyed, reverses this approach entirely. Or rather, to be more precise: the participation in the ritual celebration of comedic spirituality reveals to the philosopher or poetic thinker this truth: it is not the moral that enables grace, but grace that enables morality. This inversion of the traditional approach also requires a reformulation of the question itself: rather than asking how we must loosen the strictness of morality to accommodate the more generous favors of seemingly antimoral, gracious bestowal, we ask: how can grace be understood as the fundamental ground for the seemingly ungracious severity of law-like morality? If these two forms of the inversion—which enables which, and which must make room for which—are to be understood rather than merely noted, it is also required to realize that the universality inherent in moral law-likeness must be enabled by and hence be dependent on a more fundamental, existential universality found in the worth of being gracious and of being favored.

This is no small task. To work out the ontological presuppositions must be delayed for a later chapter. As a purely speculative endeavor it may seem so formidable as to be daunting. As thinkers we cannot overlook *our* favor: it is comedy; without this gift the Herculean task would overtax our speculative exchequer; with comedy, it is affordable. Even with the comedic art as a gift, however, the effort is not negligible, for the depth of the questioning is originary and hence is unavailable by the techniques of ordinary reflection. What must be shown is that existential worth is more fundamental than moral worth because the former makes the latter possible; and further, that our understanding of our existential worth is universal. These two points must be shown without weakening the authority of morality as absolute: it will always be wrong to abuse children, to use a person as a mere means, or to murder, rape, enslave, or debase merely to satisfy our darker wants. Yet forgiveness, as grace, may seem, if not to endorse such acts, at least to defang their censure. This is the problem inherent in the first manifestation of grace as a paradox. It is a manifestation of a paradox because we seem to need the implacable constancy of morality and yet also to need the ability to forgive provided by grace. Only comedy provides the spirit that enables us to think these two together.

SACRIFICE. The second manifestation of grace as a paradox is the phenomenon of sacrifice. To sacrifice is to bestow in such a way as to suffer, such that in giving we give of ourselves. The etymology is suggestive, coming from two Latin words *sacra*, holy, and *facere*, to make. In offering what makes us suffer we make the offering holy. Why "holy"? Originally, it is presumed, we call it holy because all sacrifices were at first made to the gods or to God, as Abel and Cain both sacrificed to God the fruits of their labor. But even without these origins the term seems apt: sacrifice makes an offering holy because no mere moral or personal advantage is served; it is somehow "beyond" normal calculation, hence is revered as something special, and the reverence inherent in such offering seems to demand some non-natural, hence super-natural realm, called "holy." Yet, even with this etymological boost, the phenomenon itself requires reflection, for it is yet paradoxical.

A child gives up his favorite pastime secretly to work hard at a neighbor's service in order to earn money to buy his mother a special gift. Learning of the sacrifice both of his favorite recreation and of the harsh labor required to earn the cost of the gift, the mother welcomes the bestowal from her son with special appreciation. The son wants his mother to know of his sacrifice, and the mother, on learning of it, expresses her heightened gratitude and love. Such acts seem entirely understandable; and yet on reflection they trouble. Why does a loving mother appreciate her son's suffering? Does she *want* him to suffer? Is this not a species of sadism? If sadism is defined as taking pleasure in another's pain, is this not exactly what the mother does in accepting the painful, sacrificial offering? Or if masochism means taking delight in the endurance of pain, then is not the child a masochist? These questions prompt a counterconsideration. Suppose on learning of her son's sacrifice, the mother rejects the gift as tainted, and scolds the child for violating a hedonistic ethics. She does this because she deems that her love for her child requires that she maximize his pleasure and minimize his pain, thus assuring herself she is not sadistic. Would this be a nobler, albeit unusual, reaction? Lest this supposition be deemed ridiculous, consider what is at stake. Do we *want* our children to suffer? Does not the mother's acceptance of his sacrifice constitute an approval of her son's suffering? How can we possibly endorse a sacrificial act? Especially if such suffering is not compelled by necessity, but merely by a desire to offer something made more precious by the fact of its painful price, it would seem morally required to chide the offerer, to teach children never to suffer willingly. Is not such self-induced suffering, as well as the warm approval of it by the recipient, the supreme folly? And if this be folly, who would be wise?

The parent who receives the sacrificial gift in no way takes pleasure in the pain endured by the child, any more than the admirer of courage takes delight in the fear and pain of one who is courageous. It is not the pain, but the offering that sanctifies. We must call this offering gracious rather than sadistic or masochistic, precisely because what is at stake lies beyond the calculus of advantage. What seems to matter here is the worth of the offerer: if I cannot give of myself, what worth is there in being me? Nobility just is the realization that who I am matters; not merely my being satisfied that matters. If I matter, and *only* if I matter, can I offer of myself. It is the mean-spirited denial of the son's autonomous worth as *offerable* that is so offensive in the second scenario of the mother's scolding her son for sacrificing. Indeed, is this not the true meaning of that remarkable tale of the original sacrifice in Genesis? Cain offered of himself, and the offering was rejected. No wonder he was outraged.

Good parents recognize that even sacrifice can be abused. A sensitive child, hungry for love, may make costly, even grotesque sacrifices, in order to win a love he feels is denied. The wise parent may point out to such a child that he need not buy his affection; he is loved regardless. These are delicate judgments, sometimes causing great anguish, just as are the judgments about when to forgive. But the fact that too much sacrifice, just as too much forgiveness, can distort beyond grace into abuse does not discredit the autonomy of either; on the contrary, such painful judgments are themselves possible only if grace already matters. One thing seems clear: if the lovers in this world of ours were offered a paradise in which no suffering, and hence no sacrifice, were allowed, they would reject it precisely because, as lovers, they would give *of* themselves and not merely *from* themselves, to their beloved. The art of comedy shows us this in a way that is irresistible.

FAVOR. Grace favors. Comedy favors. Love favors. Yet, the very nature of favor is profoundly troubling precisely because it is singular and unique, stemming from no law or principle, and hence seems entirely nonuniversal, dependent not on reason, mind, or duty but on whim, and being whimsical is highly suspicious as to its thinkability as well as its justifiability. Favor also seems fundamentally unfair: indeed, if by definition favor is unmerited, but unlike unmerited rights, is particular, it would seem unjust. One of the most torturous reflections a thinker can make is the gross unfairness of the world's allotment of favors. How can we make sense of it? That billions of human beings on this planet suffer daily under the grinding misery of hunger, abuse, rejection, outrage, deformity, poverty, and just plain lousy luck, while a scattered few have rapturous joy, beauty, wealth, requited love, fame, and health, seems a thwart to all our instincts. We do not want the world to be this way. This is not a problem merely for theodicists or theists; anyone who thinks must be confounded by it. Some of the grosser wrongs may indeed be ameliorated by social actions; but even if worldwide agencies were able to distribute basic necessities to all, there would yet be vast differences between the favored and unfavored: there is no law that can be designed to force a woman to love a man simply because he loves her and wants her to love him. If two healthy and financially sound young men both fall in love with the same woman, and ask her to marry, and she agrees, one will be rejected and one will be favored. Not all the social wrangling by ideologues will ever change that. The rejected may then suffer huge anguish, perhaps even despair. To avoid this, should we then curse favor altogether? Or would the rejected suitor, in his misery, still insist the world be a place where favor is possible? He does not want to be treated fairly; he wants to be favored; he wants the woman to choose him, not to choose both, nor to be altered in beauty so that no one loves her at all. Granted favor by definition is unfair, does it follow favor cannot yet be endorsed?

To focus on this a little less cosmically may be helpful. It is simply untrue that a favored child is always resented or envied. Her siblings may recognize she is special, want her to be favored because they love her, too. This does not mean there is no rivalry at all or that the siblings are saints; it is simply undeniable that there are special people who are radiant and lovable, and admiration rather than envy may be the human reaction. Many a child can be proud of a sibling's triumph and love her without envy. Indeed, children are very astute in this regard; they see through the fake pretense of false egalitarianism. As long as they, too are loved, it is not necessary or even possible they all be loved equally, and if parents pretend that the special child is not favored the protestations of equal love will sound hollow, and then they may resent. Why is it not possible for children to love one of their own as special? To deny this on some purely abstract principle of evenness is a deception that is always sensed and resented.

What lies at the basis of this reflection? Silvius is favored by comedic art; so are Cherubino and Arthur Goring. That they are favored by the sheer serendipity of ridiculous plots is without warrant; but that comedic art celebrates their favor is of the highest philosophical significance. Is it fair that Cherubino's naughty behavior be forgiven merely because he is sweet and lovable? If by fair we mean "even" in the sense of treating all miscreant boys the same, then no, it is not fair. If by fair, however, we mean: able to be celebrated, then yes. It is fair to favor the fair. We are never merely members of the species (the same), we are also unique (different), and unless it is possible to isolate the worth of that uniqueness, we cannot revere persons at all but only abstractions. Can we, however, celebrate this uniqueness when it is not our own personal reality? We obviously can and do—and that is the other side of grace: not the favored but the favorer. It is a point so often missed by moralists, particularly those who, like John Rawls and other contemporary egalitarians, confuse justice with sameness, and self-worth with self-interest. It is because of this special uniqueness that we can forgive or be forgiven, *and also* be favored; because of it we are also able to rejoice in another's favor and to favor. It is the last three of these that are so often overlooked.

It is comedic art that reveals this truth, and it does so by the tactic of rendering us favorers, and by celebrating favor in itself. So rendered we find within ourselves an unexpected joy at being able to favor, so that in effect we are ourselves favored by our being enabled, through comedic art, to favor. This is a great realization: we are *privileged* to be able to bestow. This ability does not come to us as an innate right, nor can we earn it; yet without it we are diminished. But to be favored presupposes a deficiency or lack and once we understand the profound nature of the lack that enables favor, we can only rejoice in the profoundest way. The lack that enables comedic favor is folly.

DELIGHT. Grace delights. It is perhaps distortive to focus on such qualities as pardon, sacrifice, and favor in terms of their seeming unfairness, for such emphasis is found only in reflection; what strikes immediately in the phenomenon of grace is what might be identified as the graceful. There is in the graceful a warm, beautiful, even sensuous joy in which the proper is not overridden but reinforced. We take delight in a ballerina's movement, the sweep of generosity of line in architecture, the joy produced by well-mannered civility, the appoggiatura or grace note not counted in the cadence, an act of abundance, kindness, or charity, and above all the ambiance of welcome sired by nobility of spirit. This is grace in its most alluring form; and since, in this form, it is so obviously worthwhile that it seems a usurpation even to analyze it. If grace delights, why say anything else? Perhaps the entire topic of this book is reducible: we go to comedies because they delight us. Period. Why say anything else?

The delight of grace, however demands analysis even more than do the other three manifestations, for the problem here is not *that* we delight in comedic grace but in what way? How can we delight in human folly? The answer seems too obvious: we do not normally delight in human folly; but we do when such folly is graced by comedic art. It is therefore not the folly but the grace, as a kind of beauty, that gives delight. The danger in this answer has already been noted: it is not the simple beauty of Shakespeare's poetry or Mozart's music or Wilde's craft, added on to a folly that delights, for then it is mere beauty that matters, and we have lost what is revealed, the worth of graced folly. The answer here must be preemptive, for its analysis must await the development of prior steps in the argument: what delights in graced folly is its truth. The graceful, as a species of beauty, when grounded in folly, delights because, as graced folly, truth matters—that is, it becomes precious to us in a very special way, open only by comedic art.

This sketch of the four manifestations of grace provides their problematic; it is now possible to discover what they mean in terms of the comedic art.

FORGIVENESS. To discover grace in its manifestation of forgiveness in comedy is not to require that comic plots or themes are about forgiveness, or even that all comic characters do indeed forgive; it is rather to identify the spirit of comedy as grounded in the spirit of forgiveness, especially if such forgiveness is of human folly. There is, to be sure, an abundance of actual forgiving in many great comedies that help to establish this truth: Gertrude forgives Robert, the Count forgives Cherubino, Orlando forgives Oliver. Portia's magnificent speech on mercy is unparalleled in its beauty and nobility; Hero's father forgives Claudio in a spectacular act of grace; Prospero forgives his brother, and even the puritanic Angelo is forgiven by the Duke. Yet, the prolixity of these gracious acts found in comedy are not enough: there are acts of noble forgiveness in tragedies, too; and Christian parables as well as Roman accounts of magnanimity also support the worth of pardon without being comedic. What must be shown, therefore, is not the mere presence of forgiveness in the plays, but the deeper spirit that enables such mercy to be seen as stemming from grace itself. This deeper spirit lies in the peculiarly comedic truth of placing the jewel of moral goodness on the cushion of human grace rather than the other way around. Yet, even with this realization, it would be a gross misreading to interpret comedic art as if it proselytizes this as a doctrine. Art never serves an orthodoxy; comedic artists do not first figure out this philosophical principle and then go to work trying to show it is true. Among the greatest of these artists there may be some instinctive, subliminal awareness of this truth, but we need not know this; it is enough that the comedic art reveals this spirit. Whether the comedic artist is conscious of these workings is irrelevant; what matters is they are there. Their art celebrates bestowal and hence forgiveness in part simply by letting bestowal *be*. In letting bestowal be, we let emerge the being of a *person*—not a creature made thinkable by rights pasted on a legatee like labels plastered on trunks; nor is a person revealed by nobler duties, telling us what to do; no, a person's essence as person is revealed by being able to receive and give beyond merit. This alone enables a person, for this alone is not dictated; it celebrates our personal, unique, and fundamental worth not because of laws or rules but because *we* matter. What must be shown is that only if we matter do moral laws and social rights have any authority at all. Comic grace is not merely the ranking of the existential over the moral, but finding in that ranking the justification for the moral as a necessary part of what it means to be a person. The first manifestation of this can be seen in the comic tension: grace is meaningless without merit as a contrast. The comedic artist is not intent on ridding us of moral restraint nor winking at transgressions against it, for only if the moral has absolute authority can overriding grace be appreciated. What is the worth of forgiveness if, in forgiving, we demote the authority of law? Is pardon spectacular if the law is defanged by mere exceptions? The comic genius needs moral authority to make grace stand out in its independence. This however, merely shows comedy is not antimoral. The present need is for a deeper argument: that grace in some way enables morality, and that the truth of this is discoverable only in comedic art. The depth of this argument can only be achieved by the intermingling or wedding of grace and folly.

Morality itself is meaningful only because we are able to do what is wrong. Why have a commandment against murder if we were impervious to whatever lures us to it, such as rage, hatred, greed, shame, and envy? Or even if we had such base instincts but were possessed of such great love and courage that resisting them came more easily than submitting, why would we need moral laws? We do not pass a law forbidding us to rework the past, simply because it is meaningless to forbid what we cannot do. But why forbid anything? Even a child senses the wisdom in having restraints on conduct that help us to be good. Morality is not merely or even fundamentally a set of rules that protect others from my selfish desires, nor is it even the safety provided me from the dangerous desires of others;

rather, it is the realization that only by willing such rules can I develop as one who matters, perhaps even: only by willing such rules can I matter at all. The truth of this—that I matter—is revealed by the exposure of my folly in such a way that this erudition is not merely another moral step, but a fundamental learning of who I am; and only if I am revealed *in truth* as a graced fool can I embrace that truth as entailing the moral law. The question then becomes, not: how can a morally responsible man be forgiven; but rather: how can a man capable of being forgiven be morally responsible? Comedic art reveals that *only* as forgivable can I be responsible. It does this by showing the truth inherent in our graced folly. The truth-revealing paradox is this: only when the grimness of automatic morality is denuded by grace is it possible for true morality to be endorsed; yet morality is "true" only if it is law-like. The very fact that comedy shows us as foolish requires that we must yearn for authority; the very fact that this foolishness is also graced, however, shows us that moral authority is authority and not mere power. This make morality more, and not less, esteemed.

Observing the tactics of great comedic artists shows us what this means. The opening scenes of *As You Like It* are not funny at all. Orlando's brother, Oliver, is revealed as cruel and tyrannic; so is Celia's father, the usurping Duke. Yet, these are not merely the necessities of plot; had Shakespeare wanted, he could have achieved the basic story line far more economically and far less seriously. What we learn from the first act is the nobility of Orlando and Rosalind, and the remarkable generosity of Adam. This is necessary for the play. We must first be shown the quality of these people, for without their radiant character, this play would not succeed as well as it does. It is precisely because they are so noble and gentle that we care about them first; their later entanglements in the throes of love-folly could not be endorsed as warmly had we not been shown their noble qualities earlier on. Yet, the first act is not precomic, it is comic itself. Even in distress the nobility of Orlando is irrepressible; it emanates like a palpable thing so that the injustice of Oliver is all the more resented. Orlando's boldness with the ducal usurper in manifesting pride in his father, thrills; and his stunned muteness—"what passion hangs these weights upon my tongue?"—amuses us in part because he is so worthy. It must be noted here that these moral qualities are not the simple negative restraints prohibiting certain actions; they are embraced and endorsed as likable virtues, so that the artist is showing the beauty of goodness and not the mere chafing of restraint that characterize moral prohibitions. Showing virtue to be beautiful is part of comedic art; not all the wild hijinks in Arden can offset this glow enkindled by the first act.

Moral laws, however, of themselves do not seem gracious at all. Their very form, as Kant points out, is imperative; as such they seem magnificent in their isolation from all human warmth. Without this inoculation against milky sentiment, the authority of law as law is jeopardized. Is not the cold indifference of law its greatest strength? Why else is justice painted or sculpted as blind? Unless the commander is given the power to demand unquestioned obedience, no army can succeed against a foe that does possess such authority. Parents are ill-advised to explain their authority, for there are times when the child needs to be told without explanation. These realizations make it seem highly unlikely that law—especially the moral law—can be sired by grace. Yet the very fact that these cases show the necessity of law's seeming indifference to persons is offset by the realization that, as persons, we can and do demand laws. It is not simply grace, but foolish grace that authorizes our submission to the formal. It is not merely folly but graced folly that spots the need for formalizing authority to save us from being merely foolish. If our instincts for gratification and self-deceit are strong, there must be something stronger to offset them, so that civility and truth can emerge. It is, after all, persons who reflect on this; it is not some nonpersonal, raw power that forces obedience on us externally. The key here seems to be that some sense of self-awareness is essential for law to be endorsed; but comedy alone denudes our self-deceit in a way that allows for the worth of persons to emerge.

To say that grace or comedy enables morality is not to equate them: nothing in the virtue of grace nor the art of comedy tell us what the moral laws are; they merely show us what it means to need morality as an essential part of our nature. Morality by itself, being law-like, reveals us merely as obedient; morality joined with grace makes us family members obeying, not out of fear or even respect for the law because of our reason, but out of love. The linkage of morality with grace does not alter the law-like authority of law nor change what the laws are: it shows rather that laws themselves are given, bestowed as gifts. They are given to show us how to be good, but being good is not the result of adherence to law but a condition for law to matter at all.

Great comedy manifests this triumph of the graceful in myriad and often subtle ways, but there is no doubt among the experienced audience that this loveliness, this sheer gratuity that delights because it is so generous, plays a fundamental role in comedic success. What is less obvious, but still palpable, is the enabling necessity wrought by the graceful that makes morality precious rather than merely endured. The moral law merely obeyed, however, is not true morality, but only its propadeutic; it is when we welcome its law-likeness as our own that it becomes truly moral.

A hint of this is found in comic form: the lover is first ensnared with the comic passion of longing; the success of the lovers is then imperilled; the lovers are finally united in sacramental union. Marriage as an institution is embraced as the ultimate resolve, for so sanctioned, the folly of love can be contained. What does this marital ending to most comedies mean? That "they live happily ever after"? Comedies are not fairy tales; neither the comic artist nor the comic audience is naive: neither Robert Chiltern's marriage to Gertrude nor Mozart's Countess, married to the philandering Count, attests to the guarantee of marital bliss. We are not even certain if Phebe truly wants to marry Silvius; even less are we sure Cherubino wants to marry Barbarina. Yet, ceremonially, the entrance of Hymen at the end of the play is far more than a mere convenient exit for the players and audience. If marriage is no utopian institution nor guarantee of happiness, it does not follow however, that it is without meaning. We can speculate about matrimony throughout the tonnage of tomes, the darkness of theology, or the ethics of promising, but it is the guidance from comedic genius that provides our keenest need: marriage is the culminating act of foolish loving: not in the sense of putting an end to it, but in rendering it coherent. Without the marriage feasts that grace the end of comedy, we would be left with mere magic rather than sacrament. It is not naive to recognize the sacredness of matrimony even if it lacks bliss; it would be naive to trust continually in the magic of Arden or Prospero's island or Oberon's forest. Even when the promised sacrament is not fulfilled, as in *Love's Labors Lost*, or when its blessing is imprecise, as in *Così fan tutti*, the reality of wedded union always lurks behind the magic as a trustworthy, realist event. Holiness replaces magic, but both are yet gracious. The law-likeness of the marital oath replaces the ephemeral promise of lovers, at which, Rosalind says, Jove laughs; but though both, being promissary, have moral authority, they stem not from law but from love. What we learn, however, is not that the "illusion" of the love-chase is enabled by the institutionalization of the union, but that the grace of magic makes way for the grace of the holy, thereby transforming morality from mere obedience to reverence.

We cannot forget that the denizens of Arden are not all happy there; we the audience are. The prenuptial lovers are in huge anguish, especially Silvius. What the loving fools on the stage yearn for is the final act, which is why, though we would linger in Arden, it is fitting the play be short. Thomas Mann is correct in his critique of Wagner's *Meistersinger*: it is far too long; comedies must be brief. Their brevity relies on their form: the lovers are eager for a settled, formal union: gambolling in Oberon's enchanted wood may suffice for a summer's night—the shortest night of the year—but the magic is, in the last analysis, not of our world; we have our own spirituality where, if not miracles or magic, at least sacramentality provides a glorious closure of the portal to love sanctioned by law. What the comic visits to these lands of enchantment do is twofold: first, magic itself—either in love potions or by love itself, as often beguiled as abetted by the cunning tactics of the fools—removes us from the banal and pedantry of pre-love; second, it replaces the magical with the sacred or institutional, thereby returning us to the nonmagical; but now it is accounted with the radiance of redemption. In this procedure we become prepared as lovers and fools to greet, perhaps for the first time, the authority rather than the mere power of the law-like. For us the audience it is not the marriage that provides the comedy but the comedy that provides the marriage. In the comedy we learn the intoxication of love, a toxicity that renders us foolish and giddy, but rather than judging this inebriation as contemptuous, we realize it as a sacred Dionysian rite, one that is holy just because it is truth revealing.

There is a further way to suggest the comic as the origin of embraced rather than merely obeyed law. One of the more precious gifts of comic spirituality is the bursting of pomposity and self-importance, two ills that darken any and all authority, leaving it mere power. Lysander and Hermia flee the "harsh Athenian law," which, curiously, the King himself suspends at play's end; the grim reign of the puritanic but proper Angelo in *Measure for Measure* is pardoned by the returning Duke who chides himself for his slackness; Shylock is saved from the strict requirements of the Venetian law that Portia reveals. These last-minute resolutions are troubling however, for they seem to suggest license or at least excuse. The comic effect, however, is not rebellion, but endorsement. Ridding the court of puritans does not lessen but strengthens the authority necessary for effective governance. That this riddance may be accomplished by well-meaning but goofy fools such as the Dogberry constabulary simply reinforces the power of comic folly. We are watching a play, after all; we are not sitting in a civics lesson. The truth is deeper here; and what its depth reveals is that graced folly staunches the hemorrhaging of raw power from the wound of authority with the bandage of welcome. Only when we are able to embrace our own folly blessed by grace can we greet the need for law as surging from our togetherness; no longer merely obeying, but honoring, perhaps even loving, it. We do this as participants in the comic ritual, not merely as observors *of* the comic presentation. That this welcome may occur only in the greatest of comedies is not a mark against it, but, given its huge import, may be a mark for it.

SACRIFICE. The rather lengthy reflection on grace as forgiveness makes the remaining tasks easier. The problematic of sacrifice consists in seeming to want the lover to suffer. Just as forgiveness is prolix in comedies, so too is sacrifice. Arthur is willing to sacrifice his marriage to Mabel to protect Gertrude's honor; Susanna and the Countess sacrifice their own safety to help Cherubino escape; Silvius sacrifices his own advantage by helping Phebe in her effort to woo Ganymede. Perhaps one of the more radiant examples is the sacrifice by Antonio in *The Merchant of Venice* for the sake of Bassanio: this is singularly gracious because the nature of his love for the younger man may be unacceptable to him, causing him to be sad without knowing why. The mere listing of sacrificial acts within the plays is less important, however, than the joyous spirit that such sacrifice seems to echo in the comedic art. If the problematic of sacrifice is eased by the realization that our acceptance of sacrificial bestowal is not based on our wanting the giver to suffer—which would be perverse—but to allow the giver to be able to give of himself—which enables nobility—the truth of this is clearly inherent in the essence of comedic strategies. Yet, it is not the endurance of suffering that is essential for comedic sacrifice but its connection to the sacred. It has already been noted that the structure of many comedies is the shift from magic to sacrament, specifically, but not exclusively, matrimonial. This shift now deserves further reflection.

It has occasionally been dreadfully suggested that the existence of actual magic in many comedies serves to lighten the play by disbelief; since we do not believe in magic we cannot believe in the play, and this reduces the comedy to fluff and nonsense. The point of comedy thus seems to be the unserious; it is escapism from the grim problems of everyday life. Tragedy, by this rubric, is meaty and worthy of thought; comedy is distraction, and anyone who writes a book on the subject is giddy. Comedy is too much fun to be thought about. Magic cannot be thought about, so comedy, insofar as it relies on magic, is likewise a mere bauble of entertainment. Such dismissive reading is unworthy, for if it is true there could be no such thing as great comedy, and Mozart's and Shakespeare's creations, being great, would simply not exist. But they do exist. They not only exist, they often rely on magic to make them as great as they are. The fallacy lurking in this obscene suggestion—and I beg no pardon for the pun on the dramaturgic meaning to "obscene"—is the plerophory that "realism" is the only access to truth. Realism, in the sense of being life-like or in the uglier locution, "true to life," is of course an impediment to truth, not a condition for it. How, then, are we to think about magic in comedic art? How are we to think about it in any art?

There is a curious quality about the magical in art. Thomas Mann points out that the love potion given to Isolde and also drunk by Tristan in Wagner's opera is unnecessary. They are already in love. The magic of the potion is thus an intriguing device to uncover what is already true. We can note similar cases. Does Eve really need to eat the "magic" apple in Milton's *Paradise Lost*? Is it not true that Eve, in her internal discourse with herself, has already profoundly discovered the knowledge of good and evil? Her reasoning already renders her unfit for paradise; the apple is a mere symbol. Or let us take a child's story: Walt Disney's charming film *Dumbo* tells of a young elephant with elongated ears who is given a magic feather by a kindly mouse, enabling him to fly. One day Dumbo lets the feather slip out; but by now he can fly without it. The magic feather was a placebo. Do we really need the magic juice of Oberon's wild flower to show us how fickle love can be? Do we need Ariel's magical tricks to force the shipwrecked villains to confront their own guilt? Or, to put it in another way, is not love itself always "magical" in the sense that it seems beyond the principle of sufficient reason, yet it brings about one of the rarest resources of self-understanding just by its power to confuse us? It may seem that, given magic, anything can happen; but great comedies in which magic occurs always show us that magic itself is entirely inept before the powers of love or sacrament. Magic in art is curiously anti-magic.

Yet it cannot be dismissed. Consider what is truly magical. In *A Midsummer Night's Dream*, Oberon, talking to Puck, spies the two mortal lovers coming through the forest. He says simply: "I am invisible." *And we believe him*. The power of dramatic language is here truly magical: four little words accomplish an entire metaphysical miracle. How easily we accept the invisibility of Oberon! How do we understand this? To understand it we must distinguish magic as a putative causal science the rules of which are simply unknown, from magic as an aura in which the serendipity of favor is accepted uncritically. In this latter sense, there is as much magic in the forest of Arden, where there are no Merlins, Prosperos or Oberons, as there is in the forest outside Athens. In comedy it is not the mechanics of magic that matters, but the enabling of favor by some preternatural coherence. Curiously, then, magic is more "scientific" than sheer serendipity, for it merely asks us to accept cause and effect on a higher plane, thereby relieving us from relying too heavily on sheer luck. There is "magic" in the power of language—which is why we can "believe" Oberon telling us we can't see him when we do see him. Such magic is rendered acceptable, however, only as a species of ritual, which prepares us for the true power of sacrament. Magic thus becomes a dramatic device to instil awe and wonder, thereby enabling both favor and reverence.

What does this have to do with sacrifice? There are two meanings to this term: 1. Enduring pain or loss as a species of giving *of* oneself, usually in an act of love, and 2. Rendering something holy. The significance of magic is relevant for this second meaning. To say magic is replaced by sacrament is to say the *device* of favoring prepares us for the *essence* of favoring: holiness. It is thus more precise to speak of matrimony than marriage, for the latter is a civil where as the former is a religious ceremony, and sacrifice in its etymological sense is religious. Yet, once we realize that sacrifice in the sense of enduring pain is coherent only as a species of loving, the connection between the two meanings is established, making the two meanings one. Once we see that sacrifice is a *loving* endurance of pain that makes sacred the giving of oneself, we can more easily see why the marital ceremony completes the comedic art.

FAVOR. Both forgiveness and sacrifice have been revealed as ways of favoring. Grace favors. The supreme act of graceful favoring is love. Comedies, as opposed to farces, are about love. Yet, love, as supreme favor, seems dangerously unjust or at least non-just, since equality and love are simply incompatible. Silvius loves Phebe, for all her faults, and no one else. In his love for her he sacrifices, he forgives, he becomes foolish and ridiculous and silly; but he does this only for her. Under the intoxication of Eros, Silvius favors Phebe. She is special. In the problematic of favor it was noted that we the audience are rendered by the sacramentality of the artwork into favor*ers*, which rendering itself make us favor*ed*. The underlying profundity of the problematic thereby becomes a truly ancient one: the one and the many. How can there be any universality in what is unique? Comic love seems entirely ambivalent in this regard. On the one hand, Puck's anointing the lovers with the juice of Oberon's flower seems to provide the answer in favor of universality, for both Lysander and Demitrius change their passions wantonly from Hermia to Helena, suggesting it is not whom we love but the state of being in love that matters, and this state is the same for all lovers. On the other hand, Silvius's devotion to Phebe and the Countess's devotion to Mozart's Count seem to show us that love is of one person only, and is made all the more glorious by the beloved's lack of worth. Is love universal? It seems it must be so. Is love not the triumph of the unique? It seems it must be so. Are these two ascriptions incompatible? We do not think so even for a moment; and the reason is because love is a species of concrete universality: we learn what it means to love (universally) by means of loving only one to the exclusion of all else (particularity). What is easily overlooked in this formulation, however, is that the lover not only particularizes his beloved, but idealizes her. It is the ideality that allows Orlando to see in his own, singular, one-and-only Rosalind the wondrously, universally, feminine. Another of the rare rhymed passages in this play shows us this. Orlando enters alone:

> Hang there, my verse, in witness of my love,
> And thou thrice-crowned queen of night, survey
> With thy chaste eye, from the pale sphere above,
> Thy huntress' name, that my full life doth sway.
> O Rosalind! these trees shall be my books,
> And in their barks my thoughts I'll character
> That every eye which in this forest looks
> Shall see thy virtue witness'd everywhere.
> Run, run Orlando; carve on every tree,
> The fair, the chaste, and unexpressive she.
>
> (III, 2)

The last line is a triumph, for in the simple pronoun, "she," we hear not only Rosalind—Rosalind and no one else—but every she there is: what it means for there to be shes. It is both intensely particular and wonderfully universal at the same time. This universality is that accomplished by idealization, and human love is the finest species of idealization possible. Yet, it is still the particular that is loved: Orlando loves Rosalind; he does not love any other woman.

To favor is not merely to particularize, but to treat in a special way that honors, pleases, and delights only that one person being favored. In this sense, favor is not universal at all, nor is it fair. Fairness is the supreme concern of justice, and hence the concrete if flawed device of justice, the law. To realize that comedic favor is unfair assures us that law and justice do not exhaust the range of what is good and noble. Egalitarians always seem to have difficulty with this, as do puritans. All of us must be deemed equal under the law; but in matters of the heart, equality is not the sovereign. Attempts to reduce love to law or law to love will always fail; even attempts to make them compatible are misdirected, if by compatible we mean rendering them nonconflictive. They must, however, be endured somehow within the same world, or more specifically, within the same person. It is comedic art that reveals this truth; it is not comedic art, or any other human activity, that removes the paradox. This ongoing and irresolvable conflict between the legitimate demands of equality in law and justice and the legitimate but unequal power of favoring in love is the deepest realization of our folly; it is, in fact, the ultimate ground of a folly that not only can, but must be endorsed. The celebration of graced folly that endorses this welcoming of both is comedic art.

DELIGHT. Grace delights. To suggest this dissembles by excess of modesty; it is akin to saying the Pacific Ocean is a bit wet. Grace is the supreme delight. Not all the urgency of gratified lust, the easing of appetite, the triumph over the inimical, or the enjoyment of pleasure, if they be entirely sundered from grace, can equal its power to delight. On its profoundest level, the delight in grace, both as recipient and giver, is joy, the kind celebrated in Beethoven's Ninth Symphony. The legitimate need for deep analysis and critique, requiring enormous concentration and effort, should never be allowed to distract us from this realization: grace, particularly as it is manifested in comedy, provides joyous delight. The nature of this comic grace is discovered in rather subtle ways, and the following observations on Shakespeare's dramatic poetry may seem rather finely drawn, but it is that very fineness that deserves our reflection. If any dramatic poet knows his craft it is he, yet the sheer power of his poetry may distract from its dramaturgic success. A few comparisons between tragic and comic passages may help reveal his singular comic genius.

When the ghost of Hamlet's father tells him how his brother, Claudius, killed him, he says:

> And in the porches of mine ears did pour
> The leprous distillment—
>
> (I, 5)

It is not only the imagery, but the meter and diction that is so remarkable. Notice the three p's, echoed by the triple hammers of the d and two t's in "distillment;" one can almost hear the popping and crackling of outrage surrounding the sinuous, serpentine "leprous," evoking the slimy entrance of the fatal "juice or cursed hebenon." The passage as sheer *sound* tells us of the sneaky, cowardly murder. It also intones a sense of solemn but diseased ritual, a quality found throughout this play, but in no other. It is magnificent poetry; but what is more: it is even more splendid dramaturgy. Listening to it we are forced to confront the truly evil manner in which Claudius slithered like venom into the royal bed and throne of Denmark. The passage tells us not only what happened, but how to think and feel about it.

Contrast this passage from *Hamlet* with one from *King Lear* in which the king curses Goneril:

Into her womb convey sterility!
Dry up in her the organs of increase;
And from her derogate body never spring
A babe to honor her! If she must teem
Create her child of spleen, that it may live
And be athwart disnatur'd torment to her!

Here again the imagery takes us within the living body, but in a radically distinct way. The consonants still click and snap, showing the passioned outrage, but in a cadence of entirely different form and purpose: we hear not alien intruders sneaking in like leprous slime, but the natural organs misfiring so that "teem" and "spleen" conjoined suggests what is natural but awry; "sterility" and "derogate" are hostile terms, preparing for us the ultimate curse in the magnificent trio of sequent words "athwart disnatured torment." The overall effect is not merely a curse, but a curse turning the natural into the unnatural—and what else are Goneril and Regan but unnatural, natural daughters? Unlike the metric diction of the ghost, there is no eerie sense of usurpation, but rebellion in nature itself: it portends cataclysm. Hamlet's ghost tells of a singularly personal evil; Lear's curse portends a cosmic evil.

It is not always the obvious tools of meter, image, and diction; for this poet nothing about language escapes his use, even simple syntax. Lodovico, in *Othello*, is amazed at the savagery Othello uses against his wife, and says:

Is this the noble Moor whom our full senate
Call all-in-all sufficient?—Is this the nature
Whom passion could not shake? Whose solid virtue
The shot of accident nor dart of chance
could neither graze nor pierce?

(IV.1)

The inverted syntax is powerful, allowing "shot" and "dart" to coincide metrically with "passion" and "shake" in the prior line; it also achieves by its inversion a wondrous effect, for its very strangeness echoes the disbelief inherent in his question; and at the same time, the syntax allows his "solid virtue" to be cleaved *verbally* from his resistance to "graze" and "pierce." The simplicity of "whom passion could not shake" is for us a touched irony, so palpable it is like a physical thing. This is enhanced by the rarity of its meter—it is not pentametric—making the lines stand out as surprising just because Lodovico *is* surprised. In this, as in the first two, the poetry becomes a part of the drama itself and not a mere addendum to it.

Compare these three brief samples from tragedies with the following two-part passage from a comedy:

> . . . thou remember'st
> Since once I sat upon a promontory,
> And heard a mermaid on a dolphin's back,
> That the rude sea grew civil at her song,
> And certain stars shot madly from their spheres
> To hear the sea-maid's music.

And then, shortly later we hear:

> I know a bank whereon the wild thyme blows,
> Where ox-lips and the nodding violet grows;
> Quite over-canopied with lush woodbine,
> With sweet musk roses, and with eglantine:
> There sleeps Titania sometime of the night
> Lulled in these flowers with dances and delight,
> And there the snake throws her enamell'd skin,
> Weed wide enough to wrap a fairy in:
>
> (II.2)

In both of these, Oberon is simply telling Puck where something or someone is; nothing more profound than that. This citation then may seem a counter to the persuasion that it is dramatic, for what does it add to the scenes, as the poetry from the tragedies obviously does add to the dramaturgy? This, we might say, is simply lovely; we like hearing it, but it does not play any comedic role; it is sheer poetry.

That it is beautiful is true. That, being beautiful, it is "merely" poetic, is false. It is dramatic, first and foremost, in creating the magic so necessary for this play to be accepted; it also tell us a great deal about Oberon: he is truly a spirit "of another sort." But most of all, it is gracious. For this passage positively caresses us. The caress is not only poetic but dramatic: it evokes magic, wonder, and sensuous awe. If one reads it aloud its gratuity enchants us. Why a mermaid on a dolphin? Do we really care what obscure scholarship might tell us about myths? Or is it enough to sense that mermaids and dolphins are simply the sea's finest denizens of grace and sweetness? Why measure the snake's enamelled skin by its breadth sufficient to wrap a fairy? What gentler measure could possibly exist? The language itself becomes a dramatic gift, and receiving it we are blessed.

To some extent these four selections are sufficient in themselves; the trust is the reader will hear these passages and sense the difference between the three tragic and the one comic, and feel the warm grace of the latter. These are all very famous citations, intimately familiar to most who are acquainted with Shakespeare. They obviously stand out: we remember them passively if not actively, for they are Shakespeare at his best. On this level the commentator has very little work to do, except to make sure he does not get in the way. I do not want to press: if the reader does not or cannot hear the grace in the comic passage that distinguishes it from the glorious power in the tragic ones, no analysis will ever light the fire of that discernment. For those who do hear it, however, the present usage of the term *grace* as characteristic of comedic art is here presented on the highest authority of all. Comedy, as art, reveals to us its participants with the necessary truth of our graced folly. As participants of any bestowal, we must be gracious in our reception, that is, grateful. But as thinkers we now must ask: what is the nature of that grateful participation of comedically revealed truth?

VII

PERFORMANCE

IT is a curiousity and a disappointment that Shakespeare's plays rarely translate well onto film or video. This may be due to the dominance of language in his dramas; the screen is more a visual than an audial medium. Even so, the rare successes of filmed versions are almost exclusively among the tragedies; filmed versions of his comedies are disasters. Why should this be the case? It would seem otherwise; films can produce magical effects impossible on a stage, the antics of fools can be heightened by special effects, and the need for interruptive scene changes can be eliminated altogether. Film audiences are far more ready to laugh at the slightest provocation than stage audiences, and the huge sea of sitcoms on television has trained its observors to spot all the buoys of the ridiculous, bobbing on its waves. It would seem, then, that, particularly the zanier comedies such as *A Midsummer Night's Dream*, should adapt well to the format of film.

Devotées of live performance argue eloquently that nothing can compare to seeing real, breathing, human actors on a stage; it is more realistic, they say. But is realism the key? Film can show mountains, bears, forests, and automobiles far more "realistically" than mere painted backdrops. Indeed, one of the glories of films is their ability to show us directly the awesome power of nature. Consider the success of a David Lean film, showing us the vast expanse of the desert in *Lawrence of Arabia*, or the endless sweep of winter tundra in *Doctor Zhivago*. Such delights are not possible on a mere stage. These points may make the devotée of live performance shift his ground a bit: it is not realism, he now amends, but imagination; precisely because we must imagine the horse's hooves wounding the earth makes it more dramatic. Perhaps. But the devotée cannot have it both ways: is it realism, which induces receptivity, or art, which induces imagination? If live actors are more successful on stage, why are not "live" horses better on film? Perhaps the point is this: only people are live on stage, all else is imagined; on film, nature is realistically presented, but people are thereby rendered merely as other visual entities. The expanse of desert distracts from Lawrence the man; the moving camera focuses on action rather than thought. Great plays focus on the human, not on nature, hence live performances are superior to filmed ones.

If it is mere imagination or mere language over sight, it might be argued that reading a play rather than seeing a live performance might be even better. This, however, is surely wrong: those whose sole access to Shakespeare is the book are missing something important: the playwright wrote his plays to be performed. The textophile is far likelier than the frequent playgoer to render absurdist interpretations of dramas. It is wonderful to read Shakespeare, of course; but it is not comparable to seeing the plays acted on stage. Curiously, it is far more important to see the comedies than the tragedies, for much of tragedy is interior anyway, consisting of reflective ruminations on the plight of the agonized hero; but comedies are ensemblic. Perhaps it is this ensemblic essence that is thwarted by film: we must always see Bottom with his crew, the fairies surrounding Titania, or Corin and Rosalind overhearing Silvius and Phebe. The powerful effect of the closeup, so dear to film directors, sabotages this communal vision, forcing us to look at the actor's face rather than the actor in the midst of others. The trouble with these suggestions is that they can be amended. Do we really think a director who avoids closeups will thereby produce better films of actual plays? Or are these rather casual remarks concerning performance merely skirting the deeper issues?

Mention of the director and the actor focuses on a far worthier problem. All performative arts are metaphysically troubling in a way nonperformative arts are not. Unlike painting, sculpture, architecture, novels, gardening, and drawing, the art works that actually take place and happen provide special challenges to the thinker. In the first place, they apparently require a second artist—Jasha Heifetz playing Beethoven—which complicates the analysis. Is the interpreter an artist? It seems churlish to deny it. Insofar as he may be an artist, however, perhaps we should not characterize him an interpreter, for he may bring something to the art work that the original artist did not provide. To suggest this is fraught with peril, however. If we say Heifetz brings something to the violin concerto that Beethoven did not, we might then protest that Heifetz has distorted the work or usurped the composer's authority. If, to avoid this charge of usurpation, we say Heifetz has merely succeeded in realizing the full wealth of Beethoven's genius, then why call Heifetz an artist at all? Neither suggestion seems adequate.

In the second place, the necessity of an interpreter brings special metaphysical static to the airwaves of aesthetics. What do we do with the uninterpreted objects of communication? Is the written score of the concerto, lying on a shelf, an art work? Can a musician read the score and assimilate the art equally with one who hears it played? Can readers of the plays be said to have experienced the genius of Shakespeare equally with one who witnesses the performance? Are there in fact two art works, the one found on the written page, the other found only on the stage? We obviously can appreciate different actors rendering different performances of *Hamlet*, with each being considered legitimate. Yet, we also can recognize someone who performs Hamlet badly or even falsely, rejecting it entirely. Thus to admit the legitimacy of variant actors' interpretations does not commit us to radical relativism; but if this is so, how are we to understand the limits? Furthermore, is the mere reader of the play to be considered an interpreter? Can there ever be an uninterpreted Hamlet? What is the relation between the written script and the staged performance? These questions are not unanswerable; that is, they are not tossed up like skeptical confetti, persuading us to abandon all thought because they are unthinkable. They serve here to remind us that the comedic art work as a species of drama cannot be disjoined from its performative essence: to be a comedic art work is to be performed. All of these fascinating and legitimate problems or even puzzles must remain a source of distraction until and unless we first address the crucial phenomenon of performance itself. Or to put it in other terms: such questions as those raised above are both interesting and legitimate, but they will never be properly resolved until and unless we first work out the more fundamental phenomenon of performance.

The essence of comedy is not merely graced folly, for this wonderful combination occurs beyond the arts as well. We are therefore required to refine the suggestion: comedy is the *performed* synthesis of grace and folly, in which the performance itself, as that which links folly to grace, is an instance of truth. Part of the worth of comedic art is, according to this suggestion, the joyous learning of truth inaccessible in any way outside the dramatic phenomenon. Once the depth of this suggestion is fully grasped, the various puzzles noted at this chapter's beginning can be resolved with authority, and not left merely to feelings or insights. Comedy, *as performed*, reveals. We therefore must consider critically what it means to say that performance is an essential part of the comedic art's power to reveal truth.

The term *truth* provides the first theme. As Heidegger has shown, truth never simply *is*, the way gold is in the mine; rather it occurs; it is an event or phenomenon, the singular peculiarity of which is that, as a phenomenal event, it reveals. It is therefore not somehow "imbedded" in propositions, as Bertrand Russell insists; even less is it a property lurking within an entity, as we might say that mass is a property of a lump of clay. What, though, does truth reveal? We cannot say truth reveals the truth, for the second use of the term in this articulation simply brings us back to the property or entity notion of truth. What is revealed by or through the phenomenon is meaning or essence. Heidegger is not so doctrinaire as to deny that ordinary usage of the term *truth* can and does refer to what is revealed as opposed to the revealing itself, nor does he even deny that we can properly say that sentences (or propositions) are true. His analysis suggests, however, that these latter two meanings are derived, and hence of lower rank. What he call propositional truth (correspondence) is legitimate, but it presupposes what he calls ontic truth (the true coin as opposed to the false coin); and both propositional and ontic truth presuppose the fundamental meaning of truth, which he calls, in *Being and Time* at least, ontological truth, which is understood as uncovering or revealing the meaning of being or existence. To say that comedic art is, as performative, revealing of meaning, is to rank it as a species of ontological truth: it is true because it reveals what it means for us to be graced fools and hence it reveals what it means for us to be at all.

Heidegger is helpful here. His distinctions make it easier for us to see what it might mean to insist that comedic art is truth only as performed. Yet, it is not merely to Heidegger that we should look in order to catch the deeper meaning of performative truth.

In Book V (475–476) of Plato's *Republic*, Socrates discusses with great care the kind of education necessary to help one become a philosopher, and hence a ruler of the *polis*. This is not to be confused with the earlier, moralist education of the warriors, which has received the bulk of criticism and analysis. Rather, the interlocutors in this passage are seeking to spot those among the already trained who exhibit a certain love of learning, called the "philomathes"—*philo* = love; *mathes* = learning. An analogy is made between lovers of such things as wine or boys who, as lovers love all wine or all boys, with the lover of learning who should not be "finicky" about his passion for learning, but love all that can be learned. The fiery Glaucon protests that such an account is too broad since it would include the "lovers of spectacles," *philotheamones*. Curiously, Socrates hesitates to dismiss these, for he says the genuine lover of learning (*philomathes*) is indeed a lover of spectacle (*philotheamones*); to wit: one who loves the spectacle of truth. The context makes it clear that the "spectacle" here refers to the Dionysian festivals, at which dramas, dancing, singing, and other rites are performed. The lover of learning, *philomathes*, is not a mere bookish scholar, but one who can and does learn from these cultural spectacles that infuse into the eager youths the Greek "ethos." What distinguishes the mere lover of spectacle from the lover of learning is the ability of the latter to absorb from the festival the universal (forms); that is, "seeing" (as spectacle) not only the beautiful thing but *seeing*—not abstracting—beauty itself. This passage is often overlooked or misread. That there can be such a thing as the "spectacle" of truth alone is richly suggestive; and that the spectacle in question is the Dionysian celebration is more so. There are many scholars, particularly in the English, epistemic tradition, who continue to read this passage as identifying the lover of truth as one capable of abstraction. But this prejudice is counter to the whole spirit of this, and other, passages. We do not love abstractions; though we might love this particular woman in such a way as to learn what it means for there to be women, or even what it means to love. Two questions need to be asked: why, when Socrates discusses the lover of wine or boys as loving all kinds of wine or all kinds of boys, does Glaucon then object on the basis that this will allow lovers of spectacles? And: why does Socrates insist the true lover of beautiful things must love beauty itself? Glaucon refers to the Dionysian revellers precisely because these celebrations were considered an essential way of educating the young. His reference to the festivals is therefore not a mere analogy. In other words, the following is *not* the proper reading: just as some young men go to the festivals solely because they delight in the spectacle and thereby miss the educational and religious purpose of the celebration, so too the thinker who merely spots that something is beautiful without understanding beauty itself, also misses the true meaning. To read the passage merely as analogy leaves out why Glaucon uses the phenomenon of the festival as the analogic comparison. Further, in Socrates' example, it is not accidental that of all the forms he just happens to select beauty. Beauty is never merely conceptual. We must not only think, but *see* beauty itself: that is what love enables. Indeed, the Greek word for "form," eidos, stems from a visual imagery: it is what is seen, like a shape. More importantly, beauty is loved—though the abstract concept of beauty is not, any more than the abstract concept of a monster is frightening, or that knowledge of the principles of light refraction tells us what it means to experience the color red.

The festivals were religious as well as cultural sacraments; one did not merely attend, but participated, as in a celebration. In this participatory celebration, the young men were expected not only to see, but to learn directly by entering into the ritual. They were thus lovers of learning. Socrates is unwilling to be as harsh as Glaucon in rejecting the lovers of spectacle because of the intimate link between spectacle and the truth as spectacle. To see the spectacle merely as a beautiful thing and not to see beauty itself is a characteristic of a dull wit—someone who is like one who is asleep—and hence not a true *philomathes*. Therefore, the point is not that the apprentice philosopher goes off somewhere and cerebrally reflects on the spectacle; rather he *sees* more profoundly. What he sees, however, is not a mere event, like a cloud passing across the sun, but a spectacle, something that excites the passion and stirs the soul, thereby making it a religious experience. Only by such passionate (or "loving") seeing—which as passionate becomes celebratory—can the participant become a true lover of learning (*philomathes*) and hence become a lover of truth (philosopher).

Among the events that make up the festival are the dramas; and they include comedy. One impervious to the comedic art is therefore not a true lover of learning and consequently not a lover of truth as a spectacle. Notice: the spectacle itself is loved; it is not suggested that the spectacle is a mere vehicle or occasional way to uncover the "more important truth" lying beneath the approach: the truth is in the spectacle as loved. This is the only way to make sense of "loving the spectacle of truth." I do not love truth independently of spectacle. Even the philosopher outside the cave loves the spectacle of the world emerging by the light of the sun, the "shape" of the "excellent." Truth could only be understood as a species of identification were it merely seen as something to be recognized, rather than "loved," and hence understood in its essence, if it were nonspectacular.

What is the spectacle of drama, specifically comedic art? In drama the spectacle—that which is seen in such a way as to delight the seer—is a story unfolding. Comedic unfolding is of lovable fools curiously immune from the dangerous consequences of folly by sheer whimsy of plot. This necessarily perceived unfolding reveals, by means of the temporal unfolding, our own being favored, and not merely the characters envied for their being favored. To delight solely in the spectacle without its truth is, according to Socrates, like one who dreams: a dreamer is one whose vision is of the unreal; the wakeful is one whose vision is of the real. To see a mere silly plot presented as spectacle is non-Dionysian; it may even create a sense of envy, in which the observor (no longer the participant) sees only the undeserved escape, and hence learns nothing about himself. Such a viewer either is distracted by nonsense or ridicule, and deems the comedic hero either as contemptuous because he is a fool, or with envy because he is lucky. The lover of such resources of learning, however, as participant rather than mere observer, becomes favored and favorer. This self-realization of one's own graced folly is learned *only* as an unfolding story or drama. Part of what is perceived, therefore, is the spectacle of our own unfolding learning: we delight not only in seeing the goofy antics on the stage; we also delight in the transformation occurring within us. We delight in being revealed ourselves as graced fools, for we do not merely see Cherubino escape, we endorse it, thereby favoring his folly (for being a lover) and his grace (for being saved). This favoring in turn favors us. We therefore do not merely see a spectacle happening on the stage, we feel the spectacle within us reveal our own reality as a favored fool, and with this revelation we discover a deep and wondrous wisdom.

The comedic spectacle takes time; and the actual temporal development is crucial. Because the spectacle occurs or happens—that is, it has a beginning, middle, and end—it reflects our own temporal and hence finite existence. What makes time endurable is suspense, surprise, and change that improves our state, or ennobles our existence. As has been noted, the ultimate triumph (Silvius finally weds Phebe) is not and cannot be the result of merit; yet neither can the change from unsuccess to success be arbitrary. There must be something about the fool that makes us feel that, though he has not merited success, it is nevertheless somehow fitting or charming or likeable that he succeeds. The most palpable of such winners is obviously the lover, particularly the young, eager, likeable or even lovable, lovesick fool unashamed of his folly since it is based on love. But there is also the other person, who likewise has not merited success, but whose plight seems to warrant the bestowal, and that person is ourself, the celebrator of the Dionysian ritual.

Comedic suspense may actually be more intense than tragic suspense; and part of the reason for this is the atmosphere of accepted fate that truly great tragedies develop from the very onset. A supreme example of this is Chorus in *Romeo and Juliet*: we are told right away that both lovers will die. Comedies rarely have introductory choruses—although Christopher Fry presents an intriguing possibility—nor is there inevitability in their pathos. Do we really care who links up with whom, Demetrius and Lysander chasing both Hermia and Helena? Surprise is far more an element in comedy than tragedy; yet this is fitting, since the very giddiness of the plot enhances favor. In tragedy it is the very inevitability of plot that enhances our ranking of meaning over success. Both surprise and suspense are characteristics of a story that unfolds based on the shared performance of graced folly. What, though, surprises? In comedy, the surprise is that folly can be winsome and that grace, as a cheat on justice, can be endorsed. This surprise, however, is also linked to suspense, not only in the sense of ignorance as to the outcome, but also in the sense of suspension between things, as a bridge suspends between the two banks. Hanging between the two safe banks, we are in suspense in a double sense: the insecurity or uncertainty of our position, and the connection between the two solid shores. These two shores can be seen either as total knowledge and total ignorance—we are always suspended between the two—or total innocence and total justice. We cannot let go of justice; but neither can we let go of our existential worth, the origin of which is childlike innocence. This suspenseful surprise is the true ground of comic laughter.

The Dionysian festival, after all, celebrates precisely that demigod who links the human with the divine. The Dionysians are not Olympians, but neither are they worshipers of mere mortals. It is this linkage or suspension between the finite and the infinite that allows for true celebration, rather than mere dutiful obeisance. Celebration, as opposed to mere prayer and sacrifice, is that species of worship that exults as it exalts; it lifts us up beyond the mere dreariness of the world, yet it does not avoid or dismiss the frailty of our humanity. This religious celebration is the ultimate origin of modern performance. Performance must be seen, just as the festivals are seen and not merely conceptually analyzed; but the seeing is of a special sort, namely the seeing in which beauty, and not mere beautiful things, is confronted; where truth, and not mere correct opinion, is embraced.

Performances not only take time, they also take place; that is, they occur *in* a place. It has been already noted that comedy is ensemblic; but this gathering is not merely on stage but in the audience. It is difficult to appreciate a comedy alone. Unlike some dramas that can be quite successfully viewed on a video screen sitting alone in our living room, comedy seems to beg communal audiences. This is not due merely to the fact that laughter is contagious—although the ensemblic community of a comedic audience may be the true resource for understanding why contagion is a part of mirth—rather it is due to the public ritual inherent in both grace and folly. We want to share our joys, sequester our sorrows. Performance unites. Even the most sour misanthrope, as long as he has not been diminished by total hate, can feel the community of ritual in comedy precisely because nothing gathers quite like shared folly and shared favor. Tragedy, as a part of the Dionysian festival, also is performed before an audience, but the reasoning for this is quite distinct. Comedy is communal in a more immediate and satisfying way.

Performance as essential for either of these two Dionysian dramas evokes a certain critique of our contemporary education that may here serve as a supporting insight. Consider what happens far too often in our universities. Eager students show up for a seminar on tragedy. They carry under their arms various texts: Aristotle's *Poetica*, Nietzsche's *The Birth of Tragedy*, perhaps a collection of essays on the theoretical basis of tragedy. A poll quickly reveals, however, that not one of these students has ever seen a live performance of a tragedy; one or two may have seen a film version of *Hamlet* or *Romeo and Juliet*; a small number may have read a tragedy in high school, usually *Julius Caesar*. They are proud of this. They do not want to see a play—that's for drama majors only—they want to be armed with multiple theories. Theories of what? Certainly not tragedies, for they must be seen. They study theories of dreariness or fate or nihilism or any other ism that is itself theory, so that in effect they study theories as theories. Indeed, the prevailing view is education based on multiple theories in order to assure open-mindedness, so that the more theories the better, lest one theory be appraised as superior to others. Their own experience of tragic art is never even considered for the simple reason they have no such experience.

The dire effect on these unfortunate lovers of texts rather than lovers of spectacle is grim. Suppose one of them, now armed with several complex theories, attends a performance. What he sees now is of course a working-out or filling-in of a system; he "appreciates" the play as conforming to a set of theoretic rules. He may even become an expert on *Titus Adronicus* by its conformity or lack of conformity to all the theories he has read. Such hegemony of theory over spectacle is an inversion of truth; it is also very, very sad.

The necessity of performance as spectacle in comedic art raises further question. Perhaps all truth is spectacle. Certainly if truth is learned and learning is paradigmatically festive—the Greek youths learned to be Greek by means of the festival—then we have a basis for thinking of truth in an entirely original way. Far more exciting, however, is the suggestion, enabled by these reflections on the Dionysian spectacle, that truth is truth *only* when it is loved. The point of this would be that truth *as* truth, and not merely as correspondence or actuality, is spectacular, and must be embraced *as* a sacred ritual in order for it to be at all. Thus, truth would not *be* without its lover, just as a husband would not be a husband unless he had a wife. This may not be as fantastic as it may at first seem. What we call propositional truth after all occurs only when there is an actual proposition, and unless the proposition has an independent metaphysical status not requiring a thinker, such truth would not be without someone to say the sentence or think the proposition. Certainly, if truth is correspondence, it would have to rely on the thinker and the thing thought, otherwise what would correspond to what? If the inner meaning of an event or an entity is made available only by the thinker's passionate affirmation of it—which is not entirely impossible—we might suggest that truth is truth only when it is loved. Plato seems to suggest this at times, identifying truth as available only to philosophers. Truth would then necessarily be linked to beauty—for the Greeks understood love as formally entailing beauty as its proper object. This heightened suggestion need not be defended in order to appreciate its significance. If truth as truth occurs only when it is loved, then the love-fest of the comedic event as truth revealing would require performance. An essential step in becoming a lover of truth would thus include becoming a lover of graced folly as manifest in the ritual. The philosopher would have to belong to a comic audience.

To speak of a philosopher as a lover of truth seems to imply there is truth first, and then some of us learn to love it. Perhaps, though, it is the other way around. Only when there is a lover is there a beloved; only when there is a husband is there a wife, only when there is a philosopher is there truth. This does not render truth whimsical or arbitrary any more than wives are whimsical simply because they depend on being married to a husband. If truth is correspondence or uncoveredness or coherent authenticity, there must be a mind that corresponds or an essence that is uncovered or a thing being what it purports to be. If there are truth-lovers, perhaps their being lovers enables the truth as lovable. Nonphilosophers would then be seen as concerned not with truth but with the shadows of it, or with the spectacle merely as amusement and not a spectacle that enables learning. If the philosopher, in his love of the truth, is somehow closer to truth, it would have to be that he has attuned himself to the *lovability* of truth, which would have to be an essential part of truth, otherwise philosophers would only love *lovable* truth and not all of truth. What, then, makes truth lovable?

The comedic art celebrates our loving the truth in the realization that we, as truth enamored, are foolish and favored. We are not philosophers merely because we can recognize that we are favored and foolish, but because what it means to be favored and foolish *as lovers* is spectacular—we love the emergence of this truth in the spectacle. Loving, which favors, and folly, which when celebrated leaves us aching for what we lack, are not idle or incidental characteristics of who we are: they are the very special characteristics that reflect our essence as persons. The question that must be asked is this: why does such truth need the spectacle provided by comedy? Surely, one might protest, I do not need to have attended comedies in order to love the truth. Surely, even if we admit that being foolish and favored are essential to our reality, such wisdom that might reveal this to us could be learned in ways other than attending a Dionysian festival. There are many wise men who realize the profound truth of our folly and our favor who have never seen any drama, aren't there? And if there are those who possess this wisdom then the comedic art is not essential.

Merely to express outrage at a shocking view does not thereby render it false. There are, of course, softer versions of this. Perhaps being in a culture in which great comedies occur suffices for a sensitive thinker to pick up on the emanations of the comedic spirit without the actual participation in the sacrament; or perhaps there are analogic experiences, though not precisely comedic, that somehow give us the same wisdom; or perhaps an acute observer of the human scene can see on his own the mixture of grace and folly, and thereby realize on his own all that is provided by the art form. These softer versions may contain some validity, but their very softness defangs their authority. Suppose we entertain the notion that only the strict version is correct: without actual performative celebrations of comedic art, the wisdom each performance provides would not be available by other means. If this were so, our tradition of performing great comedies would be sublimely precious. It would be a sacrilege to lose it.

VIII

TRUTH IN ART

BEFORE performance can be lifted to the level of celebration, the nature of truth as revealed only through art must first be studied. The term *studied* is singularly apt, for there is neither need nor intent to provide a fully developed theory. Further, the word *study* suggests a twofold approach, including both an analysis of historical figures and reflections on the actual concrete experience of the phenomenon. The claim that art is a fundamental resource for truth—particularly truth conceived as constituting some sense of essence or ground of meaning—has a long and impressive history, at least as far back as Plato, and enshrined in transcendental critique by Kant. But it is Schopenhauer and Heidegger who have given it such remarkable attention in the last two centuries; a brief sketch of the contributions of both of these thinkers should, then, be considered later in this chapter. The phenomenon itself, however, deserves prior reflection.

It is difficult for those who confront great and profound artworks with a certain degree of reverence and even awe, not to be moved by them in such a way as to warrant the claim that they provide truth. Emotivists are convinced that such aesthetic experiences provide merely personal, psychological responses containing no veridical worth at all. Indeed, the very intensity of the experience convinces these reductionist thinkers that the phenomena are enjoyed as private and unique feelings that have no universality about them whatsoever. Not everyone is moved by the *Pieta* of

Michelangelo or the Mass in B-Minor by Bach—indeed, given the vastness of the global population, only a tiny fraction of the human species ranks these works at all, thereby providing considerable evidence, apparently, that their appeal is provincial and culturally discrete. Even among those paltry few who have actually witnessed such works, not all have been moved by them; some have even found them repugnant. This sociological fact, though overwhelming, does not seem to ruffle one whit those who do esteem them. Their reaction, if they feel a need to respond at all, is usually of the genre that the vast billions who do not appreciate these works are simply—and unfortunately—missing something. Only a tiny few realize the epistemic impact of quantum mechanics, but this in no way invalidates the knowledge that such a science offers those who can understand it. And so the argument goes on as it has for more than a thousand years: does disagreement about art suffice to show art is not universal and hence of little concern for those seeking truth? It is enough for our purpose to note that nothing in the quarrel prohibits the possibility of art providing truth; Kant's analysis of the aesthetic in his *Critique of Judgment* shows how the particularity of the experience of beauty is compatible with its universality, an analysis adumbrated by Plato's account of eros idealizing the beloved as a source of universal meaning. The arguments are there in our history. What needs iteration, perhaps, is an existential understanding of what it means to see the universal in the concrete.

Direct confrontation with a great art work does move the sensitive witness profoundly. Why is this experience spotted as providing *truth*? The *Pieta* may fill us with awe and reverence, *Tristan und Isolde* may move us to rapture, *King Lear* may stir us to the level of the sublime. But what is there in awe, reverence, rapture, or sublimity that would necessitate their being true or revealing truth? Or to put a slightly different question: if Antony's speech over the mutilated corpse of Caesar communicates to us a palpable sense of outrage, why is what we learn not also available from a news video of a woman weeping over her slaughtered child outraged at the offender? Perhaps drama can reveal the "truth" of such passions, but why uniquely? Merely to ask these questions shows us the task before us: the truth found in great art is itself a special kind of truth not available outside of art. If I am a being capable of awe it is not enough to show that the *Pieta* produces that emotion, since awe is produced by nonartistic experience as well. Nor can we be content with saying that Shakespeare has keen insight into the psychology of an abused parent which he articulates in *King Lear,* for such an account suggests that the insight is available by psychological testing and hence is not unique to art. It is not even enough to suggest that this "keen psychological insight" is presented in a manner that pleases, for then the pleasure is a mere addendum. To say there is truth in art becomes a mere banal remark—there is also truth in gutter language—unless we realize that psychological discoveries and the elicitation of certain recognized human emotions do not constitute what is meant. We must revisit the experience.

We are filled with awe looking at the *Pieta*, and moved to outrage by Anthony's speech. Both awe and outrage, however, are not merely noted or recognized, nor are they merely felt as emotions in the world of nonartistic experience. In one sense they may not be awe or outrage at all, since these emotions move us to action or to resolve. Indeed, emotions and feelings are recognized as important in daily life just because they prompt action. What is the sense of outrage if it does not provoke us to seek justice or to alter social conditions to halt the occurrence of the outrageous? What good is fear if it does not compel us to run from the hungry tiger or move back from the rising tide? Artistic evocations of these emotions are curiously uncoupled from such activity. We do not step upon the stage to help Anthony punish Brutus; we simply sit there. We are moved by these passions, but do not move because of them. The passions become for us no longer a stimulus to act, but a stimulus to yield to them entirely for the sake of the passion itself. This bracketing of the practical is sometimes noted as "aesthetic distance." Just as the introduction of spices allows us to enjoy the taste of food independently of its need to assuage hunger, so art allows us to enjoy our passions for their own sake precisely because, given the distance between stage and audience, we could not intervene even if we wanted. This independence from the practical—what Kant calls "interest," making aesthetic judgments "disinterested"—allows us to focus not on Anthony's outrage as a stimulus to our desire for redressing the wrong, but simply on the meaning or essence of outrage. Why, though, does this discovery of what it means to experience outrage without being outraged, give us any pleasure at all, much less the sublime and lofty pleasure we take in watching the art work? Is it possible that perhaps the greatest pleasure consists in learning the essence of our own humanity so that truth itself *pleases*?

Aristotle points out in the very first sentence of the *Metaphysics* that "all men by nature desire to know." He supports this remarkable claim by reminding us of the most banal instance of this, the everyday satisfaction we take in satisfying our curiosity. When we hear a crash outside the window we want to look. The banality of this common curiosity is meant as an analogue to finer instances, which peaks at the learning we enjoy from discovering the truth about ourselves and the cosmos as a whole. Learning pleases. Since we learn about ourselves purely—without the prompting to action, which distracts from this purity—as we do in art, and perhaps only in art, and if learning pleases, then art pleases because it enables such pure learning. Thus runs the basic argument found in Aristotle and Kant—and it is difficult to dismiss. The task is not to dismiss it but understand it more profoundly.

It is not the knowledge itself, but the learning that delights. Furthermore, it is not the psychological fact that we emote in certain ways, but what it means to feel the passion purely, that delights. Indeed, it is not the feeling of the emotion in itself, but the learning of it *as* true, that provides the unique joy afforded only by art. Part of our elation in the artistic phenomenon of learning in this "pure" way is that we also discover that truth matters on its own. We are elated, then, by our actual being there in the audience, because perhaps only there are we palpably aware that truth as truth now matters to us, whereas before, it was truth in the service of another end, such as usable knowledge. In the courtroom we take an oath to tell the truth; not because truth matters per se, but because only by telling the truth can we render a just verdict; and thus justice matters, and truth is a mere means to achieve it. The truth of outrage, learned in the performance of Antony's speech, is thus rendered of worth to us in part because our dramatic learning of outrage is uncoupled from its normal service as a stimulus to justice. As audience we sense that the truth of outrage matters to us as much, if not more, than the purpose of outrage.

The mere presence on the stage, however, is not enough. Poorly written plays are also on the stage—that is, we are still separated from their action by aesthetic distance—and we neither learn truth from them nor take delight in them, even though they may depict exactly the same event as the genuine art works do. The temptation is thus to qualify the account by saying that the beauty of Shakespeare's poetry is also required. The term *also* is the wax that makes this floor too slippery. Without the nobility of the language the aesthetic distance becomes mere distance. Yet, the poetry itself establishes its own distancing, since people do not "really" talk that way in "real life," yet the artful (and artificial) language curiously overcomes mere distance. The perfect diction, meter, syntax, and imagery of Antony's speech, in its ideality, becomes preciously intimate to us, thereby bridging the gap created by aesthetic distance. Without the intimacy the love of learning could not occur, and without that love of learning, there could be no love of truth—as we have learned from Book V of the *Republic*. Thus, it seems there must be, in order to love the spectacle of truth, not only distancing but also nearing. The rarity of Shakespearean language ironically enables the new intimacy with the aesthetically removed passion not because it is rare or artful, but because being artful it is elegantly right—that is, we realize the perfection of revelation. Those are exactly the right words. They are not just "beautiful"—pleasing to the ear—as a part of their beauty they are also *apt.* We tend almost to nod our heads and say, yes, he's got the essence—that's exactly right. The danger here is that we might confuse aptness or accuracy with truth. Antony's words, being ideal, may show us truth, but since they are artificial—no one speaks so well in everyday life—they are not simply "accurate." We must embrace the paradox: poetic language is not common, but as ideal it provides universality no merely accurate claim offers.

The ability of such lofty language to move us without our moving is of supreme importance to us as audience because we are directly and concretely made aware that by means of the aesthetic distance coupled to the reunifying intimacy of the ideal, we find ourselves enabled to love truth for its own sake. Audiences of great dramas thus become philosophers in a sense. It is the intimacy provided by great language as universalizing that enables love, and it is aesthetic distance that enables us to put aside the practical need for action and focus solely on its truth. Only thus can we meaningfully say we love the truth. To say we love someone is to say, among other things, that being in the presence of the beloved brings us joy. Thus, to say we love the truth, as a phenomenon that reveals our essence, is to take joy simply in the presence of this phenomenon. Just as Silvius protests that he wants simply to be in Phebe's presence, whether she chide or no, so we want to be in the presence of our own unfolding, shorn of its practicality; since being in its presence gives us joy. Were the art not a resource of truth it might possibly be admired for the technical skill required to bring it about, but it could not be loved.

The "admiration" for the "skill" that brings about the phenomenon is insufficient to warrant our joyous love of truth; but the fact that art works are man-made is not incidental. Natural beauty, such as that recognized in sunsets, waterfalls, and roses may also delight us, and some might even urge us to see in these aesthetic experiences a phenomenon of truth happening. Perhaps. But even if natural beauty reveals truth, it is not the same as art. The song of the bird, though lovely, is not music; the panoramic vista may exult us, but it is not a painting; watching a noble person suffer may evoke our awe at his courage, but it is not a tragedy; laughing at the antics of a lovesick adolescent is not the same as delighting in comedic art. Somehow, truth in art requires the dependence of the art on human creativity; although curiously, to be rapt in a great play usually does not entail our focus on the dramatist's technique. Why must art be art-ificial? Is the fact that the play *As You Like It* is made up, and therefore is not "real," merely the reinforcement of aesthetic distance? Or does the origin of art as coming from our own species play a distinctive role in its being truth-revealing? There does seem to be a distinctive role, but how are we to understand it? Perhaps the reasoning can be seen along the following lines: the artist's creation lies not in his construction but in his seeing; a great painter is not merely a skilled draughtsman but one who sees the essential in the midst of the merely visual; a great musician hears truth in sounds, rather than using sounds to make truth; a great dramatist confronts the human story as it unfolds, by-passing the practical concerns of this temporal development. When artists craft their vision into an actual work, it is their vision they produce, not the object *of* the vision. In doing this well, they provoke our echoing—though inert in us until the art-experience—ability to see the essence. Part of the realization of this essence-revelation is the joy taken in our shared humanity with the original perceiver—*we* are of such stuff as these magnificent dreams are made on—and this sharing of our refined receptivity with our own kind ranks the art above nature. It is therefore not the production of the art but the prior receptivity to essentialist truth that distinguishes the artist. It is because of this priority of the artist's receptivity that we can distinguish the merely skilled craftsman from the true artist. Indeed, in some arts, there can be giants who are less skilled than mere technicians, though usually their craft is on a par with their vision. A skilled musicologist, however, need not be a great musician any more than a skilled draughtsman always makes an artist. This distinction between the artist's perception and his execution may be purely formal, for it is entirely possible that some great artists actually perceive as they execute, as Mozart obviously does with his musical creations. Whether formal or historical, however, the distinction is important, for it shows that part of our loving truth in art consists in our sharing our refined sensibility with the artist as co-member of our species. The inference from this suggestion may be a bit frightening, however, for it suggests that truth as essence-revealing is non-natural: it requires being crafted. Since what is learned in essentialist truth is our own being, and part of who we are is to craft, the dependence of truth in art on creativity seems inevitable; but it nevertheless is a somewhat eerie realization. Why must we make or craft an artwork in order to see truth directly rather than as a valuable but nonintrinsic tool for our use?

It is now no longer possible to answer this question merely by noting, correctly, that the art work as non purposive allows truth to be appreciated in itself. Now we must further realize that the intimacy with the making of art belongs to our sharing it as a craft that rips us away from nature. This intimacy allows us, not merely to recognize or even realize the truth in its being revealed, but to love the truth as needing both craft and distance. This means art must be distant in order to be near. Comedy, among all the arts, is peculiarly well-suited for this. Folly, in actual, human behavior, is a vice. Separated by aesthetic distance it can be safely enjoyed; but when shared (by graciousness on the stage as well as in the audience) in being crafted by our own making, the folly is now graced, and we embrace it as not only belonging to us but as coming from us. The enormous joy found in the celebratory performance of the very best of these is possible because its truth, as truth, is loved for its own sake. We not only learn who we are as graced fools, we become enamored with our own grace and folly being revealed. At almost every line spoken by Silvius this aching fondness is ours.

This sketch can now be anchored in deeper thought. Arthur Schopenhauer's philosophical masterpiece is one of those truly rare achievements in human history: a profound, deep, and worthy tome that is nevertheless a pure joy to read. Perhaps only Plato, and occasional moments in Nietzsche, offers any parallel. Its style is seductive; one can read it on many levels; even those not trained in philosophy can appreciate the depth and power of its wisdom, in part because it is both clear and charming. Even so, it is a prodigious work; and its length may be a bit daunting to a novice. Luckily—though I doubt if luck had anything to do with it—one chapter or section, §36, contains almost all of his philosophical vision in a remarkably insightful and delightfully written passage. The topic of §36 is genius, which Schopenhauer limits only to artistic thinking. In order to make his point about artistic genius, Schopenhauer must summarize all that precedes this passage, and most—except for his pessimistic ethics—of what follows. It is, incredibly, even easy to summarize.

Almost all human knowledge consists of perceptions—objects of our sensory experience in time and space—being connected by functions of our own consciousness. Using Kantian language, we discover that we are enabled to receive impressions of our world by what is called the sensibility; these impressions are then united by what is called the Understanding. Both sensibility and understanding are called faculties, *vermögen*, which in the German suggests the power to enable. The powers that enable us to bring the myriad elements together, both as receptor and as connector are built into the way our consciousness works, and hence are a priori. For Kant, the sensibility (which is merely that way of being conscious that enables us to receive) provides two forms, space and time; what is perceived in space and time is then synthesized in the second faculty called the Understanding by principles of connection, called categories, and for Kant there are twelve, the most important of which are causality and substance. These categories allow us to connect the temporal moments of raw sensation into a coherent, thinkable series, as when we connect the perceived wind with the perceived slamming of the door by the principle of causality, which is formally prior to the actual event. Schopenhauer simplifies this by reducing the two forms of the sensibility, space and time, and the twelve categories, to three fundamental principles of connection, time, space, and cause. Thus, human knowledge relies on this ability of consciousness to connect the multitude of our sensory impressions. The entire apparatus of making our sensations first into perceptions (in time) and then into experience (by causality, including purposive causality) is called the Principle of Sufficient Reason. What is so wonderful about this principle is that it allows us to isolate the various steps, particularly, though not exclusively, by means of the causal chain. This ability to link things together, shared by animals in varying degrees of sophistication, accounts for almost all of our success as manipulators of the world. Unlike animals, however, we also have the faculty of reason, which enables language, and which ultimately is nothing other than abstraction, which allows us to extract from a given experience its form. This power or faculty of abstraction allows us to see forms or patterns or even schemes and strategies that, being formal, are available only to those endowed with reason.

The vast majority of human knowledge is thus enabled by the Principle of Sufficient Reason. Indeed, if we restrict ourselves to useful knowledge, which enables us to control things that happen in nature, *all* such knowledge is based on the Principle of Sufficient Reason. As controllers of our world, and as manipulators of causes in events, we need nothing else. There is however, one species of knowing that is independent of sufficient reason, and that is known as "genius." Genius occurs only in art. The artist sees things and hence produces things on the basis of this nonpractical, direct knowledge that bypasses or skips over entirely the principle. But if there is no principle of connection, what is it the artist sees? Schopenhauer borrows a term from Plato: the artist knows the forms or essence—what Schopenhauer calls the Platonic Idea—of a thing. A Platonic Idea, such as beauty itself or justice itself, is the highest manifestation of the world's reality as power or world-will—hence these Platonic Ideas provide truth in the loftiest or highest sense.

Even apprentice thinkers can recognize something rare and exciting in this insight: genius skips the principle of sufficient reason. Surely, it seems, this is exactly what artists do. They do not, as scientists, take us step by step down a causal series, nor do they entertain hypotheses based on causally adequate explanations. They seem to pierce through all the normal ways we weave coherence out of the random peltings on our senses, and instinctively or intuitively isolate the central origin or essence.

Schophenauer calls this "pure" knowledge or sometimes "will-less" knowledge, meaning we apprehend it solely in its truth, since, deprived of the principle of sufficient reason, it has nothing else to offer.

Our ordinary, everyday understanding of genius seems to fit wonderfully into this account. If we ask a poet how he achieved a remarkable effect, he says he just did it, it just seemed right. If we ask Van Gogh why he used a palette knife rather than a brush to put the blob of yellow directly on the canvas we would not expect him to catalogue his motives—we say he "sensed" it would be more effective. Of all the geniuses we know about, the most obvious is Mozart, since he was writing memorable music at the age of five, and because, having forgotten to write the overture to one of his operas he sat down right there, on the day of the performance, and wrote it out in its entirety without a blot; the result was perfection. That kind of creation, we say, is inhuman. Many are convinced that, just because no human being can do such things, this inspiration comes directly from God—or perhaps, as some of his Italian contemporaries believed, from the devil. We need not bring in preternatural beings: what we call genius is that which cannot be accomplished by ordinary ways of thinking—the principle of sufficient reason. Because it nevertheless provides immediate and direct appreciation of the essence of what is represented, it cannot be whimsical or subjective: it is a species of direct, essentialist knowledge, hence it is true. As soon as we try to explain it causally we make fools of ourselves since, being direct, there are no causes to account for its production.

Why, though, is genius limited to art? Above all, it is because art has no practical value, and whatever has practical value cannot escape the principle of sufficient reason. If we insist there are geniuses in such practical fields as science, mathematics, or architecture, the philosopher would say that in those rare moments the thinker was performing as artist. Schopenhauer does not suggest this, however; he is intent on making the point that art alone is the result of genius. We take delight in art just because it is not the result of steps, although after the artwork is done a scholar may point out the elements to some extent, but never to the point that knowledge of these elements or even steps taken by the analysis of the artwork, can ever be used to produce another work of art—believing it can produces the ghastly plerophory of postmodernism in which art theory replaces art. I could study every rule, law, principle, explanation, or element found in *Don Giovanni*, join them together on different melodic structures and on a different plot, and would never produce a masterpiece. Realizing this is part of the thrill of witnessing the work of genius: for a brief moment, we too, as audience, are removed from the grim hegemony of the principle of sufficient reason, and this realization provides a remarkable sense of freedom or even elevation to the lofty.

In a passage often overlooked, Schopenhauer points out that our ability to be moved by works of genius is itself dependent on our realization that we, too, are able to partake in genius, if only passively. Hence, not even the *appreciation* of the artwork is due to principles: we become passive geniuses when the work effects us. This is a brilliant account of those who are impervious: one who hears the *B*-Minor Mass by Bach and yawns indifferently is not deficient in hearing or intelligence; such a one is simply unable to surrender the principle of sufficient reason. He takes delight solely in the success of ordinary cognition, and would rather take satisfaction in a puzzle solved by following algorithms than by truth directly felt without the mechanism of principle. That we as audience must ourselves be able to participate in genius—albeit passively—is a testament to the rigor of Schopenhauer's thinking, for he must explain not only how the artists create, that is, how they *see* originally, but that genius is somehow built into the universal dimensions of truth, which we as audience, are also capable of seeing.

What does Schopenhauer mean when he speaks of art as revealing Platonic Ideas? All representations are based on manifestations of the world-reality, sometimes called the world-will; but these manifestations are graded. The highest manifestations of world-reality are those that, like Plato's forms, manifest the essence of a thing rather than its particular occurrence within the events of the world. For Plato, the form of justice is ultimately real, and as such it enables the less real but still actual governments and men who participate in what it means to be just. The reason for saying this is that relatively just governments come and go, but our understanding of justice itself transcends these transitory states and abides eternally. The actual physical entities within the range of our possible experience—what we call "the world" in its representational sense—are nothing but manifestations of the more fundamental reality that is always conceived as the ground of meaning. Schopenhauer may well be the first major thinker to argue along the lines of what might be called the "existential inversion," which ranks the meaning above the thing. He argues, for example, that the human hand does not explain grasping but grasping explains the hand. We first are grasping beings—feral manifestations of the world will as raw power—and then, because we are grasping beings we develops hands. It is possible to see this in evolutionary terms, but for Schopenhauer it is far deeper: not science but metaphysics. The hand is nothing other than the external manifestation of the will, insofar as willing needs to take and to control—grasp. Thus, what Schopenhauer means by the Platonic Ideas is actually an existential ground of meaning: what it means to grasp is more original and more real than the hand that grasps. Genius is that species of knowledge that, ceding the principle of sufficient reason and with it the need to think in terms of entities or reifications, penetrates directly to this fundamental meaning. Both through the distancing of aesthetic removal and the nearing of intimate ideality the artist puts us directly in contact with what is ultimate, and hence what is not dependent on entities. Although we the audience are not the creative artist whose vision is originary, we are still able to appreciate the direct access to truth by our own indirect (or passive) genius. What it means to be fond of our own folly is thus directly enabled by the genius of the comedic artist, conjoined with our own passive genius to realize its truth.

The availability of Schopenhauer's critical analysis is hampered somewhat by our contemporary disdain for the vast systems wrought by nineteenth-century metaphysicians. We tend, ill-advisedly, to reject such thinkers *in toto* just because we are reluctant to accept them *in toto*. There is much to be learned from Schopenhauer—even Nietzsche admits this—however dubious his ultimate cosmology might be. In the case of his analysis of art as genius, however, he deserves greater respect, first and foremost because of the truth revealed in his analysis; but the second reason may have more persuasive chutzpah: his enormous influence on absolutely great artists and thinkers. Were one to rank thinkers on the scale of their influence on the great, Schopenhauer's image would be sculpted on the highest pedestal; for consider his inheritors: Richard Wagner, Thomas Mann, Friedrich Nietzsche, Oscar Wilde—and indirectly, through these, almost the entire artistic history up to World War II and even a little beyond that. Such heritage cannot be dismissed; Schopenhauer must have had something worthwhile to have caused such devotion in his noble advocates. Not the least among these stellar legacies is Martin Heidegger—though Heidegger rarely mentions Schopenhauer and does not identify his thought as stemming from his discoveries. The Schopenhauerian influence on Heidegger's works on art, however, cannot be dismissed by anyone who knows philosophical history. Heidegger, too, argues that art speaks essentialist truth; and both thinkers seem to blur the distinction between high art and philosophy to the point that one begins to wonder how they differ. Heidegger has the linguistic advantage of a detailed, existential vocabulary, and this vocabulary allows for further penetration into the mystery of artistry as truth.

The brief, troubling little essay, "The Origin of the Art-work" (1935), is one of the hardest to crack in the entire repertoire of seemingly uncrackable vaults that hide Heidegger's treasury. The dense thickness of the prodigious *Being and Time* (1927) is a shameless exhibitionist in comparison to the shy virgin hiding in the mists that is the "Origin." Yet it curiously elates many novice readers, even as they admit frustration, and challenges the sophisticated reader with its palpable lure. It seems so easy to read and so hard to understand. Yet its thesis is clearly stated, its arguments clearly laid out, its insights supported by truly wonderful examples—far better than in any other of his works. At first reading it seems absolutely original; yet it is in many ways not revolutionary at all. Not only Schopenhauer, but Plato and Kant are clearly discernible—and they are not there merely as foils to be rejected, but serve rather as a basis for rethinking them in existential terms. Nevertheless, the best way to read the essay is on its own terms: if much of what he says seems vaguely familiar, Heidegger would not mind at all. There is enough in *how* he says it to warrant its remarkable originality.

The thesis, as suggested, is almost too easy to state. Art, Heidegger argues, is one of the few resources for existential truth. Indeed, the essence of art is truth, conceived as a happening brought about by the conflict between what he calls "earth" and "world." In Hofstadter's translation, found in the collection, *Poetry, Language, Thought* (Harper Collins, 1971), we read: "This happening [of truth] we think of as the fighting of the conflict between world and earth" (p. 57). How, then, does Heidegger define these two terms, *earth* and *world?* The answer is very simple: he does not define them. This omission exasperates even the most loyal of readers: surely the philosopher's special role is to define his terms as precisely as he can, so that the reader at least knows what the text says. Yet, this technique is deliberate; he does not define them but he certainly tells us enough about them to realize, perhaps vaguely, what they mean. Part of the reason there is no propositional definition is that Heidegger sees propositions themselves as an impediment to the profoundest thinking. He does not, however, leave us unguided. For example: "the world is the self-disclosing openness . . . the earth is . . . self-secluding and to that extent sheltering and concealing" (p. 48). Yet, he also warns us: "But the world is not simply the Open that corresponds to clearing, and the earth is not simply the closed that corresponds to concealment" (p. 55). It is the tension or battle between them that is essential for veridic discovery. At one point Heidegger characterizes earth as "the heavy weight of stone, the dumb hardness of wood, the dark glow of colors" (p. 63). One gets the impression that earth is empirical and world rational, in the eighteenth-century sense of these terms, which come together in Kant's analysis of the beautiful, in which we see in the concrete what is law-like, and this "seeing" pleases us. This impression would be misleading if it were the basis for a "reduction" of Heidegger's existential analysis to the faculty analysis of Kant. There is much more to earth than the empirical and much more to world than the rational. Yet somehow Heidegger's depiction of art seems to echo the insights of the earlier thinkers: we think and we feel, and normally it is important to distinguish these activities, but somehow in art we think as we feel and feel as we think, so the two are brought together. For Heidegger, however, to characterize the difference in terms of the cognitive faculties is deeply misleading. Thus, the difference between earth and world cannot be seen as the difference between thinking and feeling; what *may* be similar to the earlier thinkers is the realization that art somehow brings together the familiar earth and the opening world.

Earth and world are never independent: they exist only in the conflict itself, for it is this conflict that establishes what Heidegger calls the "Open"—that enables truth to happen. Perhaps in the comedic art this Open is accomplished by the sheltering privacy of our own shameful folly being violated by the annealing grace that renders it shareable (open) to a commune of fools. The hapless Russian who beats his horse to death because he would hide from the jeering crowd fiercely wants to hide in shame, but a shamefully foolish Silvius shouts to the world his sorry plight that is the deepest joy when opened. The tendency to hide one's folly persists even as it is embraced. The tendency to hang the verses of Orlando's love on the trees celebrates a private, sheltering joy. Comedic art makes intensely private and intimate love a public, self-revealing grace. Lovers seek the darkness, which shelters; yet lovers shout their folly, which unconceals. The exquisite poetry opens up the world, the sheltering folly of the anguished Cherubino and Silvius is the earth that gives them belonging. Yet, there is philosophical folly in attempting to use earth and world as a format onto which the specific art form, comedy, can be pinned. To the comic audience, there is a felt tension—that, few can deny. To suggest that the tension is between sheltering earth and self-revealing world may illuminate the possibility that what the gathering of fools delights in is their own truth, denuded by world and sheltered by earth.

The greatest danger in reading "The Origin of the Art-Work," however, is, paradoxically, to focus too much on what earth and world "really" mean. Whatever they mean they open up a conflict that reveals even as it conceals, and this opening up is the phenomenon of truth. Thus, understanding truth is far more important than understanding earth and world—and Heidegger is quite willing to give us a sense of what this special, existential truth means without using the earth-world distinction at all. In a remarkable passage—one of the most remarkable passages ever made on this subject—Heidegger offers us a comparison. Unlike Schopenhauer, who restricts genius to art, Heidegger recognizes there are other special, wonderful, but rare experiences that also provide truth happening. In addition to the artwork, Heidegger adds (p. 62) the act "that founds a political state," and the act of "the essential sacrifice" as well as philosophical inquiry itself. Science, however, is not an original happening of truth. The reader tends to glide over these comparisons, thereby missing a rare opportunity to learn by analogy. In what way is art analogous to founding a state or "the essential sacrifice"? Forget his deprecation of science or his exalting philosophy; they are nowhere near as important as these two. The suggestion of the analogue stuns.

In what way is art "like"—that is, analogous to—founding a state? In our history the period from 1776 to the calling of the Convention in 1787 is often seen as the period of the "founding" of our state. This dating is somewhat arbitrary, of course; some might argue that the founding should reach all the way to 1865, for the Civil War wrought the ultimate coherence as an undivided nation. Nevertheless, 1776 to 1787 is that period in which we, self-consciously, went about the business of "founding" our nation. What happened then? Actually, this question is a distraction; let us turn it around. What happens *now*? A policeman wants to arrest me; I ask: for what reason? He must tell me—the writ of *habeas corpus* can be suspended only in times of national emergency. This right is not found in every state; not even in every "liberal" republic. Some academics are furious that my publisher dares to print my works. Too bad, we say: we are protected by the First Amendment. Our neighbor's children want to worship in a silly, weird religion; they try to close down the place of worship, but can't. The jurors believe the man is guilty, but do not think the prosecutor has made his case. Reluctantly, but with some pride, they must find him innocent. Every day, in small ways and in large, who we are as Americans is an inescapable part of our reality, both in good ways and in bad ways. We say: what it means to be an American is the concrete realization in the everyday, present world of what happened between 1776 and 1787. The founding established the meaning. The founding is not merely the product—the written Constitution—it is also the reasoning, the struggle, the historical forces, even the extraordinary good fortune of having on the scene men as diverse in their genius as Jefferson and Hamilton, Washington and Madison, Franklin and Adams. All these elements make up the founding. This founding is not like art at all in most senses: it is not that both are beautiful or that their products are in museums or even that both are revered. It is simply that both establish meaning as a way of truth. What it means to be American is the truth of being American, and the act of founding America establishes that meaning and hence that truth. In this sense only is the founding like Beethoven's Ninth Symphony or

Hamlet or the *Pieta*: their truth is in their unconcealing of essential meaning. The founding is analogous to *As You Like It* and *Le Nozze di Figaro*: comedy and the founding of our state reveal what it means to be concealed and uncovered as fools and patriots.

Very well. But how is art analogous to the essential sacrifice? What is meant by the "essential sacrifice"? Does Heidegger mean the soldier's sacrifice of his life for his country? Or perhaps he means the Christian notion of Christ's supreme sacrifice on Golgatha? Or is the term nonspecific: *any* sacrifice will do? If the adjective is important, what is a nonessential sacrifice? This last question seems to suggest that there are some sacrifices that are not really necessary, but others that are, and the latter are essential. This, however, cannot be what Heidegger means. The context suggests that the sacrifice, as a way of truth, reveals essence. But how does sacrifice reveal essentialist truth?

We speak of a soldier sacrificing his life for his country. Some interpret this to mean that his risky act of assaulting the enemy shows his love for his homeland. We must pause at this. Shows? A greeting card shows that one remembers a birthday, an invitation to dinner shows a preexisting fondness. What shows is always a mere indicator of something more precious; it is a token of something, a means of expressing a feeling or sentiment. The battlefield death of a young warrior far exceeds any showing. What could be greater than this offering of life that, according to this analysis, is but a mere token? The answer, apparently, is that the love is greater than the means taken to show the love. In some cases this is doubtlessly true: it is the love that enables the offering, so that the offering is a sign or symbol of the love. Hence, one legitimate sense of sacrifice is that it shows a prior affection: but this is not essential sacrifice. The harsh death of a green and happy boy wearing a uniform is not reducible to a mere sign or symbol. In rare and special cases it may be not the love that enables the offering, but the offering that enables the love. How are we to understand this? Suppose a young man has built up something very precious over the years, something he values above all else. His aunt is about to lose something she holds dear, and the nephew sells his precious collection in order to save her from losing what she treasures. Heretofore he had not been aware of any deep reverence or love for her. The act may even surprise him. The sacrifice, in this case, establishes what was not before. His surrender of what was dear, even by his own calculation, was not based on a prior sentiment—at least not sufficiently to warrant the offering—rather, in yielding his treasure a new kind or level of love was enabled. Such an experience is not unthinkable. A professor spends long hours—more than is required by his sense of duty or obligation—with a troubled student, surrendering his dinner to continue the debate, since he realizes the moment is crucial in the student's self-discovery of himself as one now able to love the inquiry. A fierce headache plagues the professor, his talk forces him to delay other pressing work, which now he must do late at night, causing him distress. He had no prior or special affection for this student before the event, but since the learning cost him so much, that student is *now* special. The sacrifice itself establishes a new relationship, so that we can truthfully say it is the offering that generates the fondness, not the fondness that generates the offering. Let us provisionally entertain this suggestion: an essential sacrifice is one in which the offering enables the fondness; the nonessential sacrifice relies on the preexistence of the fondness. Neither of these, however, should be seen as a mere sign or symbol. This suggests a tripartite ranking: from lowest to highest we have 1) sacrificial acts that are mere signs or symbols; 2) sacrificial acts that are the result of preexisting affection (enabling us to say: he sacrificed because of his love for her); 3) and essential sacrifice, which *establishes* the affection.

If it is possible for there to be a species of sacrifice that establishes rather than follows from affection or reverence, we could suggest that such sacrifice is a happening of truth, for it is an event that, as essential, enables. It is a fundamental because it is neither a mere sign of affection nor is it accounted for by affection, rather, it makes or "lets" affection happen. This is like art. Both essential sacrifice and great art do not merely reflect something else, they establish meaning, and hence they are the origin of it. Only in this way can they be said to make truth happen. The analogue of art to essential sacrifice is thus made, not to add to the list the kind of things that let truth happen, but to tell us about truth in art. The purpose of all analogic reason is to illuminate what is being studied by reference to a ratio of something we already understand. The extent to which I can understand that the noblest sacrifice *enables* devotion and is not merely an *indication* of devotion, allows me by means of the analogy to realize that art does not *indicate* something else that is true, but is an *instance* of truth itself happening.

Yet, the notion of sacrifice as an analogue to art may not be adequate to Heidegger's penetrating analysis. Consider the case of one of our national monuments: Gettysburg. As Lincoln so aptly tells us, it is the sacrifice of the brave and courageous who shed their blood on these fields that makes it holy. There is nothing in the hills around this Pennsylvania town that, in itself, sets it off as a special place—a place of reverence. Gettysburg thus provides us with an instance in which both the etymological origin of "sacrifice" and its status as painfully wrought bestowal are brought together. Few would deny that the sacrifices at that battlefield enshrine what is of the noblest dimension of being American. Yet, in the "Origin of the Art-work" Heidegger uses as an example of *art* the erection of a sacred temple that makes the god available to his people. If we see the architecture of the temple as a work of art—and who can deny that at least some temples are artworks—we also see that such erecting of a place to worship establishes and not merely shows the piety of belonging. Heidegger points out that the temple enables the sturdiness of the rock on which it rests, and gives meaning to the fleeting clouds by reference to its constancy. The temple, he says, lets the god *be*. He does not mean by this that the god is a mere creation of superstitious piety, on which the bemused modern atheist can look back with condescending fondness as parents smile at a child's belief in Santa Claus. What is enabled by the temple is not the existence of the god in a metaphysical sense but the presence of the god in an existential sense. Neither do we argue that the sacredness provided by the sacrifice of men fighting for a noble cause somehow creates the American Union—though such sacrifice surely enshrines the sacredness of the Union, which is why the place, Gettysburg, is important, and not merely the historical memory enabled by textbooks. Heidegger's profound analysis of the temple *as an art work* establishes a much firmer connection between art and sacrifice than a mere analogy provides.

In his discussion of the Greek temple as a work of art, Heidegger also mentions, briefly, the happening of the festival, which includes the twin dramatic arts, tragedy and comedy. The comedic art, therefore, no less than the temple itself, establishes or enables the historical truth of the worshipers to be made available. This may seem a quaint and even antique prejudice. History reveals that almost all of the forms of art, music, architecture, literature, drama, sculpture and painting, were at one time essentially religious, especially in the earlier equating of religion with culture. The modern critic, however, may well point out that though the arts did in fact begin as parts of religious ceremonies, it is now no longer the case. Touches of purely secular art can even be found in ancient societies—surely, some of the more lurid sexual hijinks found on Greek pottery were more in the spirit of fun than of reverence. The dominance of spiritual over the secular began to ebb in postcataclysmic Europe as recently as the Renaissance, and particularly since the Enlightenment. Is not Heidegger's reverentialist or even pietistic rendering of the arts simply archaic? Uniquely modern forms, particularly film, have no such reverence or piety at their base. Perhaps we can dismiss Heidegger, then, as mere nostalgia.

To suggest this is not to endorse it. Heidegger, after all, does not begin his analysis with his interpretation of the Greek temple which perforce must include piety; he begins with a study of Van Gogh's painting of peasant shoes. Furthermore, the apparent dominance of atheists in universities does not mean that artists are without piety and reverence. The question is not whether Heidegger's use of the ancient Greeks is nostalgic, the question is whether we learn something by studying its origins. We are attempting to understand the comedic art; it would be foolish not to note that it originates in a religious festival. The question whether that reverential piety persists to some extent even today cannot be answered in the negative merely by claiming the hegemony of the secular in contemporary comedy. There are excellent reasons to suggest there is a sense of piety in the greatest comedies, including the modern ones. What must be done is to show that the piety in great comedy is an essential part of the art work as a resource for truth. For if the work is a work because it provides truth, being true, it cannot merely be nostalgic. These reflections on comedic art as a resource for truth suggests that what makes us revere both great comedies and the battlefield in Pennsylvania is not that they are merely a part of our history, but that, as our history, they enable their truth. It is truth, then, that is the ultimate ground for reverence and piety. To understand this more profoundly, we must now reflect on comedy, not merely as a performance, but as a celebration.

IX

Celebration

A noble youth back from the wars finds himself in torment. Beguiled by the cunning of his enemy's henchmen, he has, on the basis of contrived evidence, been persuaded to believe his beloved has been treacherous. Befitting his abused honor, he has openly shamed the sweet and innocent girl, accusing her of dissembling and unmaidenly behavior in such harsh terms she has swooned, apparently fatally. Her father, outraged, has let it be publicly announced that she was dead. Due to the inept but deeply faithful watch of a goofy assortment of constables led by Dogberry, the plot of the miscreant Don John has been uncovered, and the young soldier, a friend of Benedick named Claudio, is required manfully to face the grief and ire of the abused father, promising to atone for the putative manslaughter of the girl he loved. The penalty exacted by the cunning parent is twofold: first, the youth must promise to marry an unknown kinswoman of the father; and secondly he must stand vigil the entire night at Hero's fake funeral wake. The audience of *Much Ado about Nothing* is, of course, aware that Hero is not dead at all, and that it is actually she who, in disguise, is the substitute bride. When Claudio lifts the veil, he cries, "Another Hero!" which itself is so rich in ambiguity and double or even triple entendre that it rarely fails to produce risant approval from the audience. The warring lovers, Beatrice and Benedick, join in the double marriage ceremony with

Claudio and Hero, and the knotted plot is retied into a happy knot, and all is well.

It is a delightful comedy. Sitting like a jewel on its dramatic cushion is the vigil. There is magic in this ritual. How are we to understand it? Is it a purgative rite, like the confessional? If so, is it not inauthentic, since Hero is not really dead, and Claudio had been tricked into believing that what he witnessed was his financée's infidelity? Given the ethos of the day, was not the young soldier justified in accusing Hero of treachery? Or do we, like modern lawyers, take refuge in arcane complexities: it was fitting perhaps that Claudio refuse to marry, but his condemnation was too harsh? Such hair splitting is not the stuff of great comedy. Hero was deeply abused by Claudio, even if his censure were the usufructs of deceit. In some legal sense, of course, Claudio is innocent; but so was Hero. Somehow a wrong had to be righted. It is, after all, rather magnanimous of Hero's father to wed his abused daughter to the one who abused her, however unwittingly. It is this same father, however, who requires that the young warrior spend the night in vigil and to promise to wed someone he has never seen. The magic wrought by this ritual is all the more remarkable given that the central players are not Claudio and Hero but Beatrice and Benedick. Why then, does this solemn performance at a pseudo-funeral, in one of the briefest scenes in the play, take on such dramatic import? Somehow one senses that, were the vigil excised from the drama, it would not be the great comedy it truly is.

The possibility that one might try to produce the play without the vigil is a rich and helpful suggestion. Claudio's reattachment to Hero would then be akin to a marriage counselor pointing out that since it was villainy that outfoxed Claudio's trust, Hero should forgive him. The resolution would thus be based on a pragmatic weighing of cause and effect. Why not resolve the problem in this way? It is so very sensible, so modern, so . . . understanding. It is also banal. A happy ending would be achieved by enlightened psychology, pleasing those who delight in solving puzzles, but not moving the comedic audience. There is nothing magical, nothing sacred, nothing sacramental in such a solution. Does this mean that great comedy requires a nostalgic and superstitious belief in mystery? There is nothing nostalgic nor superstitious in this comedy at all, though there might be mystery. Without the vigil the shift from Claudio wretched to Claudio delighted would occur without the spiritual atonement necessary to persuade the audience that something very important has taken place that profoundly alters not only Claudio but the whole cast—even Don John's villains—as well as the audience. The folly of Claudio needs to be graced by the sacramentality of the vigil. Even though Claudio was tricked, he nevertheless doubted Hero's honesty as well as her chastity, and his denouncement of her was brutal. To dismiss these offenses without a celebratory rite, and thus to rest solely on legal innocence based on the excuse of ignorance, leaves us bereft of the need for spiritual grace. Shakespeare is too keen a dramatist not to provide that grace. If the essence of comedic art is graced folly, we must allow the work to *be* gracious. Claudio's vigil thus cannot be seen merely as a purgative, in which he endures pain to pay for his wronging Hero; the funeral celebration as a ritual is not fake at all; it transforms us even as we know Hero still lives. The scene (in Act V) takes place within a church, into which Claudio and others enter with tapers, and from a scroll the youth reads:

> Done to death by slanderous tongues
> was the Hero that here lies:
> Death in guerdon of her wrongs,
> Gives her fame which never dies:
> So the life that died with shame
> Lives in death with glorious fame.
> Hang thou these upon the tomb,
> Praising her when I am dumb—

The entourage then solemnly chants the song:

> Pardon goddess of the night
> Those that slew the virgin knight;
> For the which, with songs of woe
> Round about her tomb they go.

To which Claudio adds:

> Now unto thy bones good night;
> yearly will I do this rite.

Don Pedro then ends the solemnity:

> Good morrow, masters; put your torches out:
> The wolves have prey'd; and look, the gentle day,
> Before the wheels of Phoebus, round about
> Dapples the drowsy east with spots of gray.

These last lines tell us that the brief scene we have just witnessed lasted the entire night. Such is the magic of drama that we feel no impropriety in this. The meter of Claudio's lament is trochaic not iambic, which is almost universally used by this poet to intone ritual and solemnity. (The homophone of Don Pedro's "prey'd" with "prayed" is a wonderful touch that lightens, as does the dawn. The word *guerdon* here means "recompense".) The impact of the poetry is unmistakable: the ritual enshrines the truth: Hero was innocent. The slanders against her were lies, the guerdon of her fame now forfeits the deceit: truth does matter, and this comedy celebrates the triumph of truth. It is not the hurtful shock that induced her swoon that is recompensed, but the falseness of the accusation, a falseness that needs solemnity to offset it, allowing truth, dawnlike, to emerge. The sacrament of matrimony, which is comedy's final triumph, sanctifies the future; the sacramental ritual of the funeral sanctifies the past by removing the profanation of deceit. The latter must be borne before the former could take place. Only through celebrations of these two sacred rites is comedic truth possible. It now becomes necessary to examine the use of the term celebration as a way of truth.

Christians speak of celebrating Mass or the Eucharist, or the sacrament of Baptism as joyous welcome; yet even requiems are celebrated, though they be sad. What must be understood is that in its truest sense, celebration is a species of worship. Yet it is also, in spite of the sadness or solemnity of some occasions, a performance of shared joy. What gives this species of worship its joyous essence? The answer can no longer be delayed, and it has been prepared by the previous two chapters: the essence lies in its *happening* of truth. We are in truth, sinners. Not for the celebrant is worship based on pretending we are mere innocents before an abstract divinity of automatic justice, or mere slaves cowering in fear before a mere vengeful deity, or automata functioning before a supreme source of energy, or even entirely worthless beings used as playthings of a godly jester. Certainly we are not celebrants because we deserve the favors of a deistic providence. To celebrate is to worship as fools, sinners, flawed lovers, penitents, and abused abusers such as Claudio. To worship in any other way is to worship in deceit. Yet, as we take joy in worshiping as we really are in truth, neither do we take refuge in our faults, as if it were a good thing to be a bad person. We know we are not entirely corrupt, for we love each other, sometimes in magnificently foolish ways, but we are not unmoved by beauty, particularly not the beauty of a noble soul. To celebrate is to worship as lovers of our own disclosing truth, warts and all. It is this honesty, this embrace of our being exposed as both worthy and unworthy, that enables joy. For as celebrants we worship without disguise—

or rather, since as fools we do sometimes beguile even ourselves, we worship as denuded in our own disguising.

The celebrant worships truth in a shared joy, and the sharing, as a truth-event is not merely the congregational sharing before an actual religious service, but the deepest sense of sharing there is: love. The paradigm of folly is the lovesick; as comic audiences we participate in that illness, from which, as Orlando says, we would not be cured. There is a radiant honesty about comedy that is almost palpable. Here we are, exposed in our most intimate vulnerability, the shameless confession of our denuding folly, and find it graced. Such joy is not possible were any deceit, sham, trickery, or disguise involved in the audience's sharing, for we seek, in this curious, perhaps strangest of all ways of worshiping, to be revealed as we are. In this sharing of our love-folly our truth not only matters, it is what we offer, as in a sacrifice, giving of our true selves and not some falsely gilded image. We can only call this the joy in truth happening.

In what way is this comedic event different from the other arts, particularly the performed? Is not Oedipus also rapt in the tragedy of his own truth taking place? Is not all art, as Schopenhauer and Heidegger labor so to show us, also based on truth? Is there not joy in the final movement of Beethoven's Ninth Symphony, a joy that happens as a truth-event? To be sure. In Oedipus, however, the dramatically suspenseful uncovering of truth is hugely satisfying, but it is not joyous; Beethoven's Ninth celebrates joy in its truth, but not as graced folly. (Though it must be admitted there are moments in the last movement of the symphony that are gloriously "comic," such as the clumsy, heavy-footed lunges of the grunting bassoons and throaty, muted brass, suggesting a rude farmer with mud-stained, oversized boots slogging into the splendid palace of the sublime.) No thoughtful listener would deny that the symphony celebrates joyously, and thus is also a species of worship. The claim is not that comedy alone celebrates, and hence worships, by offering our truth as an event. It is rather that comedy must be seen as that species of worship that joyously celebrates truth, a characteristic shared by other, though not all, art forms. What distinguishes comedy is that this celebration is achieved by folly and grace. The emphasis now is on the celebratory essence, and that such celebration is worshipful.

It cannot remain unmarked that although in some sense the truth of comedy transcends any particular faith, there are nevertheless certain religious qualities that seem necessary for great comedy. The art works used in this analysis are significantly Christian; and the origin of comedy as an art form stems from the Dionysian festival. Both of these religions emphasize the immanence rather than the transcendence of divinity; they both center on an incarnate god, with a mortal mother and a divine father. They both seem to celebrate or worship with self-recognition of human folly. Grace, however, is much more dominant in the Christian theology than in the Greek; and Shakespeare is simply a superior comedic genius to any Hellenic artist. Mozart, Shakespeare, and even Wilde are deeply Christian in their spirituality if not in their doctrine. Are these historical items irrelevant? Why should they be disregarded altogether? The Christian doctrines of the forgiveness of sins, the redemption, and above all the curious teaching that love is the nature of God's relationship to his creatures, creates a spiritual atmosphere that enables comedy in a very special way. Comedy may well be the preeminent Christian art form; and Christianity may be the preeminent spirituality necessary for comedy, especially comedic truth. It is possible now to raise a disturbing question: What enables us to reflect upon our weakness and our folly without dread? It is not the certainty that the Christian will be forgiven this or that particular sin, for that is presumption: it is the trust that comes from thinking on the supreme reality as a personal, and indeed loving, hence forgiving, father. This should be emphasized: the comedic genius never abuses his art by assigning the happy incidences of plot to a divine agency, for that is cosmological usurpation, assuming a divine prescience unfit for fools. It is quite otherwise: only as fools graced by favor can we delight joyously in our truth being exposed. To say Christians celebrate the sacraments is to say they perform them openly in a joyous way, as a species of worshiping a personal, loving, god. To say we celebrate comedy—or that comedy is a celebration and not a mere performance—is to affirm the sacramentality of the art form and hence to see it as a species of worship.

Celebration is not a private act of personal spirituality, nor is it a mere public event, as is the inauguration of a president, it is a communal act of worship that not only presupposes the prior state of togetherness but instantiates by performance the actual sharing itself. We are not first a communal audience that then celebrates the comedy, it is the sharing of the celebratory act of worship that brings us together in a new, sacramental way. What weaves the fabric of this communal belonging is the sharing of our folly as a species of self-denuding or opening that is our truth, in such a way as to bestow favoring grace on ourselves and each other; and this open sharing alone is celebration in its truest sense.

Sharing itself now needs reflection. There seem to be four kinds or perhaps even levels or stages. On the first level is the simple but compelling fact that among our pleasures are those that, being shared with another, intensify or enhance their enjoyment. This basis of sharing might be called companionship. The very nature of comedic pleasure is exacerbated by the knowing wink, the common laughter, the eagerness to talk about it afterward. A mark of this important contagion is often found in the unwillingness of the uncompanioned to attend a comedy alone, for the simple joys ring hollow when none is there to share, the emptiness becomes a positive pain, and one had as lief forego the art than to endure it by oneself. This same loner may well enjoy private viewings of paintings or music or even tragedy, but comedy can be cruel if there is none else by. The first level of sharing therefore serves as a personal delight and hence advantage to the individual sharer. The second level of sharing is quite otherwise: the playgoer cares about his fellow, and, knowing the delights of the piece, wants to share it because he also wants to please the other. This species or level of sharing might be called friendship. It is not merely that I shall enjoy the play more if I can share it with a companion, it is rather that *he* will enjoy the wonders of the art form, and his delight brings me joy. Provisionally, in this context, I shall use "delight" to refer to the pleasure taken from the experience, and "joy" to refer to the elation taken in sensing the other's delight. In order for this higher level of sharing to occur, I must care not only about what is precious in the artwork, but also about the worth of my friend's appreciation of it. We often seem to want to share comedy with a friend more than to share other art forms, in part because comedy is by its nature so profoundly friendly. The third level is an intensification of the second, and might be called educational. Here, the friend cares about bringing to his fellow celebrant not only a shared pleasure but ennoblement. The "teacher" takes his friend, as "student," to the performance because the learning inherent in the experience is simply so worthwhile he would fain not keep his friend so unexalted. This sharing as learning is possible only because truth matters and there is a rare and otherwise unavailable truth in the comedic art form. The highest level of sharing is that in which what is shared is ourselves. This is love. The many attempts to come to grips with the full meaning of love are here expanded by the suggestion that its essence is seen as the pinnacle of ranked ways of sharing. Comedy is peculiarly suited to this capital sharing because it involves the celebration of our own denuded favor.

This rapid sketch suggests the following: even outside the comic celebration, we acknowledge four levels of sharing: as companions, as friends, as co-learners, and as lovers. This fourfold ranking can be made entirely independently of comedy; but with the suggestion that comedy is, as celebratory, essentially a species of worshipful sharing, the application of this four-tiered ranking to comedy enables us to see what true celebration is. Celebration is that species of worship in which truth is shared in four ways: companionship, friendship, fellow-learning, and love. This does not mean that only when we attend comedies with our lovers do we celebrate our truth as a sacrament. Indeed, the fourfold ranking is not meant as a yardstick to measure the celebratory power of the art form at all; the ranking is made solely to suggest what sharing means. It is analogous to ranking generals, colonels, majors, captains, and lieutenants to show us what command means. If I do not appreciate the ranking, I really do not understand command or sharing.

Nevertheless, the fact that love seems to cap the ways in which we share, does suggest that the link between actual comedies and romantic plots is not merely fortuitous or incidental; and since it is NOT incidental, the hierarchy of sharing must be examined more deeply, and the first *critical* move must be a certain refinement on the lowest level, so as to avoid confusion. Parents sometimes tell their children to share something, in the sense of giving. "Alan, share your orange with Mark," means that although the fruit properly belongs to Alan he should *give* half of it to his playmate. There is much that is right in this, but it distracts from the sharing itself since we seem to focus on the sacrificial aspect. Contrast the first parental command with this second: "Alan, share your toys with Mark." In this sense, Alan does not surrender his ownership at all; he learns that by sharing the toys he has more fun. For reasons of critical precision we should excise the "giving" part from the "sharing" part of these phenomena. A friend may know quite well that an orange halved simply tastes better than a whole orange kept, but wisdom lies only in part with the sharing; the other part is the actual giving, and wonderful or even noble as that may be, it distracts. We want to focus solely on the sharing. Sharing the toys enables better play. The toys are already there; they can be played with alone or shared. Sharing them enables adventure: if Mark has a toy truck and Alan has a truck they can crash into each other's vehicles with gusto. Sharing the checkers allows the game to be played at all. It is not the giving but the sharing that matters.

This distinction becomes more important on the second level, for we do not want to know now why a friend gives a gift to a friend but why he shares something. Alan has an orange, Mark does not. Were Alan to give the entire orange to his friend we would understand that in terms of generosity and sacrifice, and such noble characteristics would blind us to what we now seek to grasp. Alan halves the orange, and shares it. Why is this an existential advance? Both delight not only in their own pleasure but in the shared pleasure. Indeed, to make this point, we can refine it further: as far as sharing as opposed to giving is concerned, it is better that both eat half of the same orange than that Alan gives Mark an apple and each enjoys his own fruit. It is crucial that they both taste the same tangy, sweet, biting citrus, for it is the sharing, and not the individual pleasures, that matters. On this second level, the sharing enables the appreciation of the other's delight, and by doing this the autonomous worth of the other is celebrated—that is, we take joy in it. What else is a friend except one with whom the delights of the befriended become our own joy, just because, as friend, the delights, and now also the joys, are ours as well? Not all the accounts of friendship based on sacrificing, psychological feelings, caring about the other's happiness and success, approache anywhere near the profound realization of the centrality of sharing. When Alan experiences the sharp-sweet explosion of tasting the orange, the realization that this wondrous feeling is also Mark's, and the elation felt just because the pleasure is one and not merely two distinct pleasures, a rare and spectacular discovery is revealed. The point is not merely that Alan takes joy in knowing Mark is pleased; rather it is that both of them are united in the same pleasure, and consequently, in the same joy. It is not merely that Alan appreciates Mark's having pleasure but that Mark appreciates Alan's having the same pleasure, and this mutual realization ratchets up the intensity of the joyous sharing that is the deepest existential phenomenon of friendship.

This deserves our reflection since it is counter to so much of what is grim and elitist about much contemporary accounting, especially utilitarianism. The hideous plerophory that making someone else happy, especially by sacrifice, is the pinnacle of love, friendship, and even moral goodness, is hereby deeply challenged. Suppose a friend sacrifices his appreciation of a drama by giving me a front row ticket so I can see the play. What a burden this places on me: I take my pleasure at the cost of my friend's? This is exactly the opposite of what I want. I want to see the play; but as friend I may want him to see it too; I would rather have two back row seats that cost what one front row seat does. He, however, denies me that sharing on some misguided feeling that his own sense of sacrificial delight should be denied me. What I want is not merely to see the play, or even for him also to see the play; what I want is to share the play with him. The utilitarian, in practice, is a tyrant, for he wants to provide me with pleasure but does not allow me to provide him with pleasure, and what enables him to provide this is his apparent superior knowledge of what causes pleasure. There are, of course, moments in which sacrifice is noble; but it is never as fundamental as shared joys. I not only care about the well-being of my friend, I also care about him caring about me. True friends understand this instinctively. Philosophers should not be blind to this. The tactic is the simple realization that sharing outranks giving, at least existentially. Comedy, as a sharing celebration, may be the deepest realization of this truth.

The single most identifying characteristic of a great teacher is joyous sharing. Since this is unquantifiable it is elusive to the pollsters and thus remains a feckless adage of mere sentiment to educational measurers. Nothing could be sillier and sadder than to overlook this, but alas, when statistical norms are taken as some sort of wisdom, what else can we expect? Just as one incapable of true friendship will continue to insist that Alan sacrificing his ticket to Mark is nobler than sharing the play with him, so educational mavens who insist that education be made easy or that classrooms are playgrounds, are those who have simply never taken joy in the hard, demanding effort of sharing truth. It is the sharing that matters. But it is not the teacher sharing his knowledge any more than it is nobler to let Alan give the whole orange to Mark. What is shared is not the known result, but the learning itself. Hence, the great teacher not only desires his student to possess knowledge after the class that was not possessed before the class, rather he shares the actual joy in learning, which outlasts and outranks the knowledge. This passion can occur in any subject matter and in no way is restricted to classrooms. Nevertheless, the paradigm is that teacher who shares the joys of cultural and spiritual learning, as in literature, history, art, religion, and philosophy, in which one's own heritage is celebrated. Such sharing is as far from multiculturalism and anthropological comparatives as can possibly be imagined. To share what is our own—the highest modality of teaching—is here revealed, remarkably, as a species of friendship. For who is a greater friend than one who lets learning happen by sharing what is our own? (What else do great comedic artists do?) Just as it is a mistake to rank the sacrifice of the whole orange by Alan to Mark above their sharing it, so it is a mistake to rank the giving of knowledge above the sharing of truth. Truth shared is a celebration. We share this truth of our own folly in the comedic celebration; but the joyous learning is also dependent on our sharing the glory of our own English language in Shakespeare's art work. When Alan halves the orange with Mark there is mutual joy in the sharing; when Alan takes Mark to a great comedy, the joy is in the sharing of truth revealed through the ritual of a common heritage and language. The sharing lets each other learn what is preciously true, and hence ranks above the sharing of the orange.

It is glib enough to suggest that love is the sharing of oneself. Indeed, if the prior paragraphs are correct, we should perhaps rephrase the sentence suggesting that love is the sharing of each other—for again the danger here is that "sharing of oneself" seems one-sided and sacrificial, whereas true sharing must always enable the other to share as well. Even with this refinement, however, the question persists: how can we share ourselves? Alan cannot cut off his arm and exchange it with Mark's. In erotic love we might suggest the lovers share each others' bodies in a venereal sense, which might prove helpful as a metaphor or even paradigm, for I do not merely surrender sacrificially my own body to another's use, but actually share it in a triumph of intimacy. We enter and are entered; our bodies are shared with each other in the same pleasure because to some extent it is the same body, so fiercely are they joined. Indeed, one might even suggest that the sharing rather than the mere taking or giving of the intimacy in a way that enables joy in each other's pleasure is what distinguishes erotic love from mere lust. Even with this as a guide, however, we must dig more deeply to discover in what sense we truly can share ourselves rather than merely giving (as in sacrificing) ourselves. This demand for deeper reflection yields an insight that may be called the paradox of sharing, which is simply that before I give I first must have, suggesting that the non-shared preciousness must be presupposed by the possibility of sharing it. Alan must first have the orange as his own before he then can share it with Mark, making sharing a consequence of prior non-sharing. Every lover realizes the wisdom in this paradox, that suggests, not as a solution—since paradoxes do not have solutions—but as an embrace of the paradoxic, that what it means for Alan to have an orange is realized only when he shares it. Even with this lover's realization, however, the initial point must be reinforced. To possess something must first be good before sharing it becomes better. In sexual intimacy I first must be able to feel pleasure before I can share the pleasure. Granted that sharing it enhances the pleasure, it still, as pleasure, must first be mine before it then becomes ours. The puzzle is this: is it the same pleasure but intensified, or is it a new and special pleasure on its own? It must obviously be the latter.

To speak of love as sharing thus presupposes the worth of each sharer *as* sharer and not merely the worth of each as pre-sharer. We now re-ask the original question: how can I give or share myself? I can give of myself as a sacrifice only if I first matter to myself in such a way that surrendering it is painful. I can share myself only if joining with the other enhances the worth of both in a new way that does not preexist the sharing. But what is this new way? What must I presuppose about myself such that I can be shared? Is there a special *part* of me I can share, reserving other parts as my own? This seems fair enough in most cases, but in love the suggestion seems horrifying: it is precisely my entirety that would be shared. Yet, the eagerness to assure myself that all of me is shared again blocks the beloved who also would share entirely. Perhaps what enables total sharing is our presence, not merely as presence but as belonging to and with the other, suggesting that what enables love-sharing is the mutual belonging of each presence so that there is a new presence, that of the unified lovers. If the hierarchy of sharing matters we must realize that this belonging of presence rises out of truth-sharing, for that was the third stage, sharing as learning, that enables the fourth and last: sharing of ourselves. When Alan halves the same orange so as to share it with Mark rather than give the whole orange to Mark we say the delight in tasting the orange itself is shared and that produces joy. When my presence is not given (as in sacrifice) but is shared with my beloved, this requires the beloved's presence is also shared with me, so that the delight taken in the other's presence now enables the joy of both presences being together. We can identify this sharing of our presence as belonging. We belong not merely to each other, but belong to the other's presence, and that just means that the offering of the lover's presence cannot in any way impede the offering of the beloved's presence; indeed the "offering" as such is a distraction until and unless it is accepted, but even this locution is faulty since it leans too much on the deepest error: that of accounting for sharing in terms of mutual sacrificing or giving. In the highest level, the language of giving and taking cannot belong at all, for it smacks of commerce. We do not give or take, we share. What we share is our presence, and by sharing it we enable a new presence, *our* presence, which establishes belonging. This presence is not a part of ourselves, but is ourselves as sharers. When Romeo catches sight of Juliet the presence of her beauty becomes the beauty of her presence. Since presence is opposed by absence, we recognize it as being near rather than away, but since presence is also opposed by concealment, we also recognize it as appearing rather than being kept secret. In sharing, then, we draw near even as we expose ourselves mutually. This self-exposure is a way of opening, and hence revealing, and so it is an instance of truth happening. Only in this careful, existential language can we seriously suggest that in the highest level of sharing we share ourselves. This highest level cannot dispense with the three previous stages, for the hierarchy itself is necessary for what we mean by sharing.

There is a danger that the detail may distract from the context. It is hugely important to understand the essence of sharing, because unless we do the suggestion that celebration is communal worship remains merely a vague provocation. With this critique of sharing we now can realize that the term *worship* is not dependent solely on its object but on its existential status as truth-revealing phenomenon. We need not ask about the nature of the god being worshiped or even to insist the audience is self-conscious of some hidden or overt religious doctrine. Celebration is the shared joy of that which unites us, performed in a public way as to enable the sharing; as such it is a species of worship. It is not that species of worship that relies on a set of doctrinal beliefs as in an organized religion, though the nature of certain religions, such as Christianity, certainly provides a spirit that enables its celebrations to focus on our truth as finite—which is what comedy does. It was noted that celebration, even of requiems, is joyous; now by the unpacking of the phenomenon of sharing we see what joy means and why it is essential for celebration. The mistake would be to take the four-tiered structure of sharing and simply apply it to comedy as if it were an algorithm providing assured steps or procedures to produce the outcome. If anything it is the other way around; though this need not be insisted. When Alan halves his orange and shares it with Mark, we note that not only is their delight taken in the same object, but the realization of the shared delights brings them a joy that can only be enabled by the sharing. The two boys' eyes twinkle as they see each others' enjoyment of the slightly messy, juicy, sparkling pleasure on their lips and tongues; they may even laugh as they see the juice dribble on each other's chins, each realizing that he is dribbling, too. Comedy is like this. We not only delight in human triumph, we also take joy in the denuding of what is most profoundly ours: the truth of our finitude revealed in folly that, because it is graced, enables joy.

It is perhaps only now that we recognize the centrality of the previous chapter. In the comedic celebration what is shared is truth. Before we could understand this it was necessary first to comprehend how art works generally and comedic art particularly provide truth on its highest level. Unless we grasp the essentiality of truth's nature, provided by Schopenhauer and Heidegger, the present discoveries on celebration could not take place. So intimate, so special, so fundamental is our own folly that to deny it or escape its sting, or to demote its ranking, is the grossest deceit. What enables this truth—the truth of our folly—to be celebrated is the grace bestowed on it, a grace revealed only by the genius of the comedic artist. This bestowal is celebrated in a species of worship that rests on sharing, so that we now can suggest that only as shared can essentialist truth be learned. We discover by this that the noble acts of sacrifice, which are usually seen as the prime manifestations of highest love, are enabled by the prior sharing. Unless I first share, I could not sacrifice. This inversion may seem outrageous—indeed, *must* seem outrageous—to those for whom morality and ethics depends solely on obligation. But for those who demand that truth is more fundamental even than goodness, the realization must be that sharing enables sacrifice. Sacrifice may still rank as the supreme *act* of love; but the *truth* of love must find in the sacrificial act the prior ranking of self-sharing. Were I unable to share, I could not sacrifice; or rather: unless I first shared the so-called acts of sacrifice would be self-gratulatory performances that burden rather than lightens the recipient. Thus even the scriptural reference is made clear: "Greater love than this no man hath than to lay down his life for his friend." The being of the friendship, as sharers of our presence, is presupposed; that already-existing friendship based on a sharing that is almost sacred or holy in its ability to unify us, alone makes the sacrifice the greatest act of love.

Comedy celebrates the holiness of this sharing; it is first and foremost the sharing in and with the audience; but it is also, on occasion, the sacred acts within comedy, above all the sacramental act of marriage. But the vigil or ritual of preparation, in which the soul is purified, also reveals the holiness of sharing. The vigil in *Much Ado about Nothing* is a healing, in which the soundness or wholeness is restored—the making whole (or holy) of the disparate and fragmented is accomplished by the sharing that alone enables celebration. For some, the suggestion that celebration is a species of worship offends precisely because terms such as *ritual* and *sacrament* provoke a sense of solemn, dutiful submission, in which the smallness rather than the greatness of the kneeler weighs down on us oppressively. Even if we admit that such ceremonies instill a sense of awe and reverence, such experiences seem antipodal to the joyous unity felt in high comedy. Whatever celebratory joy there may be in great comedy it surely is the opposite of the dreary hush of holy places. It is tempting to meet this critique simply by pointing out that true worship need not be so narrowly confined—indeed, the overemphasis on such cathedral-like solemnity may be an error in the approaches of some faiths. Before we dismiss this, however, a challenge must be made to the critique. There is a felt realization of reverential awe and solemn wonder in the comedic theatre, especially in Shakespearean or Mozartian performances. Who can escape altogether the magic or Arden or the melancholy grace of Prospero's island or the curious welcome felt in Olivia's Illyrium? The brief vigil of Claudio is a part of the play, and its occurrence in the church adds to, and does not distract from, the drama. To be sure, the dominant feeling after a performance of a true comedy is one of joyous celebration that lightens as it uplifts, and makes us glad we can share our common humanity rather than fear the reprisals that may come from the wickedness inherent in it. But this is precisely why such effort is taken to focus on Alan sharing rather than merely giving the orange. Comedy simply widens the range of what it means to worship.

Another critique must now be considered. When the home team wins the championship the fans pour out of the arena in a delirious need to celebrate. The consumption of alcohol at such times would impress any

Dionysian, but the spontaneity of their shouting, cheering, rabid antics, and feverish mania may seem entirely unlike anything we note in our celebration of comedy. It is, in fact, not very good celebration, but there is more in it than simple noise. The fans shriek, "We won." "We"? These overfrenzied, overweight, overloud and overbearing intoxicants are not on the team: they did nothing at all to assist the athletes in their triumph. The few in the stadium who cheered on the players might possibly have encouraged or inspired the team, but the greater number who watched and cheered on television certainly could not claim their yelling inspired the victory. Yet, it is right and proper to say "we won." The felt unity of fans and team, indeed even belonging to the city whose name is on the uniform, is grounded in a sharing of a common joy. It is churlish to deny their happiness or even to deny that they celebrate. But can we dare suggest this frenzy is, as celebratory, a species of worship? Perhaps not; but insofar as the felt unity among the celebrants enables not only delight among the fans but also joy in the recognized sharing—insofar as the realization that where we belong seems to take on transcendent meaning—such feeling is sufficiently analogous to true celebration that some sense of worship may even occur here, for now the felt unity with the community is, though perhaps crudely, a species of piety. It might even be pointed out that sports have no lack of ritual: watch the ceremonies at the Olympics or the World Cup or even singing the National Anthem at the World Series. It is not necessary to equate *Le Nozze di Figaro* with a local high school's victory in a basketball league, for that would be egalitarian nihilism; but it is pretentious to claim that celebration is limited only to its finest instances.

One leaving a worthy performance of a magnificent comedy may feel a variety of emotions, not all of which correspond to anything revealed in this analysis. The technique of philosophical reflection is not that of the pollster. Rather, the question to be asked is whether the accounts of sharing and sacramentality enable us to think about what true comedy is. We are celebrating beings—to be able to celebrate seems as fundamental to our existence as the ability to laugh. We are also, if given the benefits of high civilization, able to create and enjoy comedic art. The single question, as critic here, is this: is our celebratory nature connected essentially to our refined ability to make and enjoy comedy? If so, then more particularly we ask: is the phenomenon of sharing, with its fourfold hierarchy, a fundamental part of such celebration? The reflections and arguments in this chapter suggest it is, especially if we realize that what we celebrate is our folly and our grace. One final refinement, however, may be necessary.

X

Fun

THIS wonderful, Anglo-Saxon word is etymologically connected to "fond"; the suggestion that comedy is fun seems, in light of this, all the more apt, for we grow fond of our own folly, especially folly grounded in erotic, and hence stupefying, love. The usage of the term, though, is far more ubiquitous, in some cases suggesting: pleasure, sport, play, recreation, entertainment; and in less amiable uses: mockery, cruelty, insult, or simply, nonseriousness. In its adjectival derivative, funny, it even means laughable. The richness of its diverse usages, however, should not distract from its special, nonreducible meaning. Not all pleasures are fun, though some definitely are. Not all fun is mockery, though to make fun of someone is often both cruel and mocking. To suggest comedy is fun is not merely to add on another adjective that on occasion fits some plays or parts of plays but is absent in others; it is rather to suggest that fun, when analyzed in a critical, existential way, throws light on comedy as a resource of truth unavailable in any other way. The paradox therefore is that "fun," often thought as delightfully nonserious becomes among the most serious of philosophical topics. It is serious ironically because it in part offers a certain brightness of spirit and warmth of affection that offsets the bleak severity so often identified with "serious" thinking. Somehow an image has emerged of the wise as a grim, scowling, stern, pedant who shudders at the levity of the giddy. When great comedies are recognized as fun, this image must suffer eclipse. There is as much truth, perhaps even more truth, in comedy as in tragedy, and the philosopher is required to doff funereal weeds and don the raiment of cheery play—attire, unfortunately, ill-fitting the accustomed mannequin of the putatively sage. There is something funny even in this: how on earth did it ever happen that thinkers were supposed to be humorless? Have we been missing something?

The paradox reaches deeper. Armed with gravity, thinkers who address such dire topics as evil, suffering, nihilism, guilt, and skepticism have an easy time of it. They are taken seriously at the outset, and certain looseness of critique is winked at by their readers; at least they are playing—or perhaps it is more reverential to say "working"—in the right mud. Those who would address amiable, non-dire topics, however, must earn their credentials from a reluctant jury. It is easy to write about despair, but despairingly difficult to write about trust; easy to adopt skepticism, uneasy to give birth to sound judgment; cheap is the price of espousing nihilism, dear indeed to engage in the meaningful; tracts on tragedy abound, but even paragraphs by philosophers on comedy are rare. To defend this mortician's gloom it is often pointed out that these darker topics deserve our attention precisely because they are problematic: we need to explain the tear, not the smile, query evil but simply accept the good, worry about error but coast along with success. Why should laughter be any less thoughtworthy than weeping? Why should the sinner be more interesting than the saint, or the happy less worthy of thought than the wretched? The single dam that blocks the dirty torrent of these dark waters is unbreachable, because it is undeniable: there are great comedies. This fact is positively painful to the dour. Woe to the woeful—they cannot, in truth, deny this greatness. Whatever is great deserves, nay demands, our reflection and our critical thought. Fun, when properly understood, is essential for such comedic greatness, and therefore fun must be taken seriously. But is not fun non-serious? If by "serious" one means "grim" then, of course, the paradox becomes an inconsistency; but if "serious" means worthy of being asked, then the duty to inquire into fun becomes earnest; indeed, there is an importance in being earnest.

Why, though, use "fun"? Is it not too Anglo-Saxon, too vernacular, too imprecise? Any term with only three letters may seem too quaint for philosophical discourse. Its use here is dictated by its aptness: it is the right word. Whatever else it may mean, fun is not to be equated with the trivial. Mabel, in Oscar Wilde's play, is fun; so are Touchstone, Bottom the Weaver, and Susanna in Mozart's opera. The term suggests a luminous, merry vitality that infuses a cheery counter to finding in human folly only an indictment. Fun is the total rejection of nihilism; yet it is neither naive nor giddy, and certainly not optimism. Mabel is not ignorant of human weakness or flaw; she simply refuses to be outclassed by them. For all her seeming irreverence toward institutions, she is actually very serious about Arthur's proposal: she has selected exactly the right man, and has patiently waited for the supreme moment. In many ways she is far more careful than Gertrude in choosing a mate. Her wisdom, however, is not merely an additional quality; in her case her being fun is what enables her to be wise. As fun, she is a realist. Fun, however, is not merely to be found in some characters within the plays; it is rather what makes the entire play a comedy rather than a merely amusing story; it creates, if you will, a certain friendliness in the audience to the avatar of Dionysus as mischief-maker appearing on the magical stage.

This friendliness, found in the echo of fun's etymological link to "fond," deserves a special critique. It is a curiosity among friends that they endure what otherwise would be an insult. Italian American friends call each other wops or dagos and seem to take especial delight in this; German friends call each other krauts, and even blacks seem to accept the nearly profane term *nigger* when used among friends. This readiness to turn insult into fun is not restricted to ethnic or racial slurs: the nearsighted are called four-eyes; the slender, beanpoles; the hairless, baldies; actors, hams; professors (especially of philosophy) absent-minded. These epithets applied by non-friends would occasion no little violence, but among friends we say they are simply having "fun." How do we account for this? The danger is that we shall dismiss it as a mere psychological outlet. The phenomenon needs deeper reflection. Various possibilities suggest themselves.

The first suggestion is that such friendly insults constitute a form of privilege. Just because such barbs normally hurt, in the case of friends they are endured. This may be partly true, but "endured" surely is the wrong word, for both friends seem to take in them huge delight that far surpasses mere endurance. The second suggestion may be that I allow my friend to "insult" me with dreadful names because I thereby am enabled to trust he merely jests. This suggestion may be made more telling by intensification: perhaps the feign of insult *forces* me to trust him, thereby bonding us more firmly. A third suggestion might be that such seeming abuse is the taking and giving of license rather than mere privilege; that is, an allowed misdemeanor that shows the affection outreaches the sanctions. Another possibility is that hearing the insults unanchored in any personal venom against me, I learn how truly silly they really are, and hence develop a happy immunity against their sting. This fourth suggestion, however, prompts a deeper fifth: is there, in the prolixity of insult, a glitter of truth, as a tiny speck of gold winks through the gravel and sand of the sluice? Does this possibility of truth in the insult thereby reinforce the presence of grace: even were these insults warranted, coming from you I embrace them?

These are interesting possibilities, and all may be partly true. But not all suggestions are so benign. One that probably is not true at all nevertheless looms as a darker explanation. Perhaps we take pleasure in abuse as the masochist seems to enjoy pain. Wound me, dear friend, lest I rest too comfortably on the merely pleasant. Or worse: read in the scars and weals you have given me a bleeding testament to the sacrificial folly of my submission. Such reading interprets the playful exchange of insult as a species of perversion. It is an unpalatable and surely false account. Then why bring it up? It is not suggested merely to show there can be false accounts; rather, it is considered here because, though grotesque, it actually enables a truer version with surface similarities. We delight in the insult not because it wounds, but because it does not wound; indeed, it gives a non-perverse pleasure. The friendship is an armor that allows the impunity of as well as the truth of, the barbs of insult to be shared. It is not, therefore, simply that a friend gives the insult, but that in sharing the immunity of the barb—especially if there is truth in it—the friendship is reinforced by celebration. This is fun in the loftiest sense, one much closer to the fun of comedy, for it is sharing a triumph; it is a species of brightness spotlighting truth. Yet, as comedy shows us, this brightness is not deceptive; nor is the cruelty of the barb entirely anaesthetized.

Is Mabel's irreverent reverence woven of the same tough fibers as a friend's licensed insult? Is Arthur's acceptance of her stings and nettles a contrast to the deep hurt imposed by Maria on Malvolio's lack of it? It is not necessary to answer each of these affirmatively to learn the preciousness of fun. There is probably some truth in all these suggestions, though none by itself suffices; perhaps the whole list still misses all, but it cannot have missed altogether. There is a paradox in the phenomenon of fun, but if so there is light in the mist. There is, however, also a danger. Fun skirts cruelty—perhaps it is even a bit cruel itself—but we know the true from the abuse. Were the cruel not latent in the comedic it would not sting; and folly must be stung. Fun, even with its barbs, is an echo of the vulnerable innocence in all folly. Let these fools be. We prefer our Ardens to their Edens; if celestial bliss cheats us of the right to sacrifice or the boon of bright self-mockery, we prefer our mortal earth, for denied suffering and folly I cannot *offer*, and offering is the heart of bestowal and a fool's love. It may be supreme folly that without a wounded heart the deepest love could not be, but if so, we embrace this folly that lets us love, mocking our need for mere contentment. We would rather be a wounded fool than a pampered pet. Perhaps only fools can offer; perhaps this is the deepest sense of the comedic fool: bereft of skill and cunning to achieve mere possession, he rather gives than takes in a giving that is costly. He may prefer to take, but denied that, still willing to participate in offering, that is, to share, he gives; sometimes what he gives and hence shares is himself. If this be folly, who would be wise?

There is isomorphism between the puzzling phenomenon of friends insulting each other and comedy insulting fools: both are done in the spirit of fun which ranks the fondness above the sting, but leaves the sting intact. To refine our appreciation of this comedic truth, we can distinguish the colloquial usage of "having fun" from "being fun." We say Mabel *is* fun, the anti-Malvolio plotters are "having fun." In the vernacular "having fun" is often used as a synonym for enjoying oneself, or even "having a good time," which is a vile phrase. Being fun, however, seems a trait of one's character or personality, and it is this latter sense that is truer to comedy. Being friends, we insult with impunity; being fun, we mock our own folly without contempt. These insults between friends may yet have the sting of truth within them, and the self-mockery of our folly in comedy may also sting with truth; but in both cases it is the fondness that enables our being fun. With this precision we now can say that comedy is fun and not merely that comedy is a species of having fun. As members of the comic audience we may not possess those charming characteristics of a Mabel or a Susanna that make them fun; but as co-celebrants of the Dionysian sacrament, we do not merely have fun but we become fun—we share the same armor against the cruel, yet also share the same sting of the truth.

To say that comedy itself is fun (as we say Mabel is fun) rather than that it merely enables the audience to *have* fun, and thereby to suggest that we the audience also become fun, requires deeper, ontological reflection. It was earlier noted that comedy, as fun, is profoundly antinihilistic; this does not mean that after a performance we feel worthwhile; but that the comedic access to truth enables us to think through the errors of nihilism. The undercurrent of this truth has been at work throughout most of this entire essay: direct confrontation with it can no longer be avoided. That it emerges now, in the consideration of fun, may seem ironic, if not outlandish; but there seems no reason to delay it further any more than to have anticipated it earlier.

Comedy is an art form that shares its origins in the Dionysian festival with tragedy. On the surface it may seem that the latter tends to create a nihilistic attitude by focusing on death, inevitability, and failure, whereas the former is antinihilistic because it focuses on joy, life, and laughter. In truth, however, both dramatic forms are antinihilistic, but in profoundly different ways.

If nihilism is taken in its philosophical sense it means there are reasons and arguments available to support the contention that what we call our life, existence, or presence is without meaning—or to put it more directly: there is no way we can think or make judgments that are true or false about such existential topics. Part of the reason for saying this is that such topics are not approachable through ordinary ways we makes sense of things, such as causes, purposes, or even moral principles. Thus, I can certainly think about the cause of Othello's death—deep knife wounds damage the vital interior organs—or even discuss the morality of it—he ought not to have murdered his wife, so he felt morally compelled to end his own life; I can even consider the psychological states in Othello's mind that render his act purposively significant. What I cannot do, apparently, is use any of these ways of explaining things to answer the question: what does it mean for him to kill her? Or even: what does it mean for there to be someone like Othello? Such questions are not approachable by the acceptable standards of giving reasons, and hence they are, in the deepest sense, unreasonable and thus unthinkable. To say life and existence are unthinkable is nihilism. Accordingly, many forms of metaphysical reductionism are nihilistic; for if I can explain all that happens to us, as well as all we ourselves do, in terms of natural phenomena such as atomic reactions or purely mechanistic causes, then there is no autonomy to questions of worth or meaning: we are nothing but machines and everything we do is the result of physical causality.

Curiously, this reductionistic nihilism is exacerbated by those who appeal to purpose as a way to avoid the dire aridity of mechanism. When we ask, what is the purpose of our existence? unwittingly we prepare the way for our own meaninglessness: not because we do not know the purpose, or even that we may not have a purpose, but because *if* we have a purpose, then our meaning is equated with it, and we become mere serviceable elements supporting something else as a means; for the purpose of a lamp is to light the room, so that if better light is available from other sources the lamp becomes entirely useless, and as useless it has no value, worth, or meaning whatsoever. If I have a purpose then, whatever I serve is the only source of judging who I am; by myself I have no meaning at all. How then do we escape this threat to our autonomous existence? All the legitimate ways we think operate by establishing coherence or synthesis in some way: the causal series links one event to another, purpose links the motive to the act, and morality links my will to the authority of law. Usually, though not always, such synthesis is articulated in terms of applying a principle or law to a specific situation: it is the principle of causality that links together the series that makes events intelligible; it is the law that governs actions by the synthesis of its universalizability. But where is such synthesis to be found when reflecting on our existence as such? Unless there is some way of bringing together the elements of my existence, I cannot think about what it means for me to exist, and nihilism is inevitable.

Long before we were self-conscious of causal connections, we told stories. A story is nothing but a connection between the phases of time which, when told, manifest their meaning. This ability of the story to provide a noncausal synthesis of past, present, and future has such enormous power to illuminate what is peculiar to the temporality of persons that the early mythmakers or storytellers were often regarded either as divine or as inspired from some supreme agency as a person with its own story. Stories, therefore, provide an existential unity for being a person; they are indeed more fundamental even than the causal series, though the two are often intermixed with disastrous results. Stories can be either accurate or fictive, as when we seriously tell the history of the Civil War, or knowingly tell a fantasy to delight children. This distinction, however, pales in importance to the fact that stories can be well or poorly told. When the telling reaches the level of genius, stories provide, by their synthesis, a unique and direct access to existential coherence and hence nonarbitrary, existential truth. It is sometimes argued that mythmaking is the sire of science, for mythical cosmogonies can, on reflection, become cosmologies, which later become paradigms of causal, and hence testable, hypotheses, leading to science. This, I submit, is well intentioned but entirely misleading. The great and powerful mythmakers were storytellers, not causal chroniclers, and their progeny were not the early cosmologists but, quite understandably, better storytellers. In Greek thought these superior story-tellers were first the epic poets and then the dramatists. (Indeed, one might argue that both the Hebrew Moses and the Greek Homer are hugely successful as storytellers just because they are already dramatic in some sense, rather than merely narrative.) In any event, the development of drama, with amazing speed, became art works that, by their connection of plot, character, and theme, provided a postmythic resource for thinking profoundly on what it means to be self-consciously in time. As such they are the first genuine philosophical resources for truth as antinihilistic. Nihilism now reveals itself as anti-story; and in particular, anti-drama. Drama reveals the temporal unfolding of meaning by two distinct, though interrelated, ways of artfully presenting plot.

In the first case, tragedy uses the dramatic plot as an echo of fate, by which is meant that characteristic of our becoming over which we have no control and which often seems inimical both to our well-being and our ability to understand. Although the term *fate* is usually used to denote both favorable and unfavorable fortuity, in this context I shall use "fate" exclusively in its tragic sense. Through no fault of her own, Antigone finds herself torn between two valid but conflicting demands on her obedience, either of which would lead her to misery. The inescapability of this dilemma forces the audience to realize three things: 1) she is not at all responsible for her dilemma, hence her agony is undeserving; 2) the unfolding of her story seems guided by the power of inevitability; 3) her unsuccess, however, does not eclipse her worth. This third point is the greatest: who Antigone is—what it means for her to be—remains as a vivid realization even after the final horrors. Thus, the plot is in service of her character, for the plot shows unsuccess, while her character transcends it. What we call fate, therefore, is nothing else than that which is learned by the plot within tragic art: fate is to our reality as tragic plot is to drama's reflection of it.

The plot of comedy focuses less on those aspects over which we have no control, and more on the misfirings and unpredictability of human projects, which, having unforeseen consequences, take on fate-like mysteries that at the beginning of the plot may be just as ominous as those in tragedy but by the end are favorable. We need a word to replace *fate,* and the term I shall use provisionally is *serendipity;* so that just as the plot of tragedy echoes the "reality" of fate so the plot of comedy echoes the "reality" of serendipity. Silvius finds himself in a dilemma, as does Antigone: he loves Phebe, but she does not love him. As in tragedy, the audience is led to the realization of three things, similar to, though not exactly identical with, tragedy: 1) he is not responsible for this anguish; he did not choose to fall in love with her who does not return his affection; 2) the unfolding of his anguish is not guided by as strong a force as inevitability, since much of it is due to human initiative that goes awry, but there is an inescapability about it that provides dramatic coherence—and I shall shortly give the proper title to this; and 3) the anguish of his suffering does not eclipse the worth of his loving, thus making the comic plot, as is the tragic, in service of our understanding him, the character. Who Silvius is, and what it means for there to be a Silvius, thus emerges from the dramatic unfolding as a species of coherence, which is the key to understanding what it means to reason, and hence is a thwart to nihilism since it shows we can think about meaning rather than merely "give" or subjectively bestow meaning on our temporal unfolding.

Thus, both dramatic forms are antinihilistic, even as both celebrate the sheer fortuity of events, or at least our incompetence in setting up projects, that in part reveal who we are. We are beings who are buffeted about by uncontrollable forces, but we are more, for the inevitability (not determinability) in tragedy and what I briefly call serendipity of comedy do not exhaust the resources of either genre: the dramatic story does provide coherence to our existential becoming in time, but such dramatic stories are in no way reducible to their plots, especially not those elements of plot that are divorced of all human selection, tragic inevitability and comic serendipity. These two notions now deserve our attention. Tragic inevitability is not at all akin to metaphysical determinism, since it is not fundamentally based on causality at all; rather, it is a characteristic of the way the story is told. Great tragedies are presented in such a way as to produce in the audience a palpable sense of fitness or even logic to the development. Although we admire Antigone, perhaps even grow fond of her, and certainly do not want her dreadful end, when it comes there is an inescapable realization that any other ending would be somehow false. Poorly written dramas with sad endings lack this sense of inevitability; indeed, they often irritate us precisely because the artificiality of the death leaves us with a cheap sentiment of mere sad frustration. This inevitability, however, is not, as so many critics seem to think, due to some metaphysical or mythic belief in capricious forces or mysterious motives of literally personified weavers of destiny; rather, it is entirely the product of craft or art: it is due to the way the story is told. The plot of *Antigone* can be presented by an ungifted writer so that no inevitability is felt at all. Sophocles, however, somehow sensed that, were the characters of Antigone and Creon developed in certain ways, the inner logic of their unhappy end would follow as a result of the coherence evolved by the weaving, not of actual metaphysical forces, but of art. This inevitability is thus entirely aesthetic, and not cosmological; and being aesthetic it provides us with truth and not mere opinion or belief, and certainly not with scientifically established causal connections. This tragic inevitability is the result of genius; it does not tell us why things, especially unlikeable things, happen; it tells us what it means for them to happen. Perhaps the most important of these discoveries is that, in spite of her unsuccess, Antigone's nobility still matters. Who she is, what it means for her to be at all, is not eclipsed by her wretched end. Any cheap moral lesson, or post-terrestrial reward, or cosmological theory, detracts from the enormity of this learning. The inevitability of her story is required for this truth to be learned.

Is there a similar "inevitability" in comedy? Yes and no. It is not as powerful as inevitability, which is why I briefly suggested "serendipity;" but that term is borrowed from an entirely different vocabulary, and can no longer serve. It now should be obvious, especially given the title of this chapter, what we properly should call it: fun. It is fun, not tragic fate, that provides the inner coherence of a comic plot, rendering it thinkable. This makes fun a species of fate in its widest sense. Though this may seem a somewhat unusual suggestion, the way for its emergence has already been learned. We must ask in all seriousness: how must we understand comedic fun if it is to correspond to fate in tragedy? When we reflect on the profound work of the comedic artist in revealing not only characters that are fun, such as Mabel, Susanna, Orlando, and Beatrice, but also the way of being fun that is the gift to the audience, we learn something of what this might mean. When we watch Bottom reflect joyously on his dream-like adventure with the fairy queen, what amazes us is his robust, even cheerful, acceptance of it, for all that it is troubling; when Mabel won-drously accepts Arthur's proposal she does so in the embrace of all their faults, his as well as hers; when Orlando agrees to allow himself to be "deceived" by the "boy" Ganymede, we realize his acceptance of the ache that such pretending brings. There is, in fun, a creative "letting be" of that which the unfolding of life's mysteries offers. This "letting be" is not, however, mere acceptance of things as they happen: it is creative in the sense that art is creative and not in the sense that the mere putting together of elements, as a carpenter puts together a bookshelf, is "creative." It is closer to the creativity of good parents letting their children be or become who they are, which is the opposite of simply letting them choose or discover what they like. Dramatic artists let their characters be, which means they do not force them to fit their preconceived notions, but neither do they simply say whatever is convenient: they must be consistent. Many great artists have recognized that in some sense they have little control over the emergence of their characters, and have even confessed their subservience to this emergence. Mark Twain confesses the tragic element of *Puddn'head Wilson* came about in spite of his attempt to write a comedy; Wagner admits the death of Isolde was forced upon him by the inevitability of the myth and the emergence of the music; Verdi, Mann, and Wilde have all noted similar phenomena in their work. We the audience share this fun as letting be only when our participation in the art is celebratory; for we must also "let" the ceremony be by a most active engagement in it.

Fun as "letting be" cannot be the mere realization that we do not entirely control our destines; it must also be courageous. All of them: Bottom, Cherubino, Mabel, Claudio, and Rosalind—they all embrace their folly in a courageous way. To some extent, this courage is a thwart to certain traditional accounts of comedy, for it has been argued that tragedy is the arena of the noble, leaving comedy to the base or common. Nothing could be farther from the truth. There is great courage in being able to embrace our folly—which even we as audience do in celebrating it—and courage is an essential quality of nobility. Does this mean that comic characters are noble and hence heroic? Do we genuinely want to speak of comic heroes? Is not the cowardice of Falstaff part of his comic essence? But Richard II is also cowardly, yet noble: it is confronting our cowardice that enables nobility. Comedy may simply be more denuding of our flaws: what renders the flaw coherent with the courage is the weaving of them together in what we call fun.

There are few things as beautiful as human courage. Watching a young girl such as Juliet accept the dire plan of Friar Lawrence is a part of her beauty; watching another young girl, Hero, face up to the demands of her father's cunning is beautiful to watch, just as we cannot but thrill to the beauty of the young soldier's frightening valor. It is necessary, as thinkers, to distinguish the moral from the aesthetic, the good from the beautiful; but it is also necessary to see how they belong together. Kant's argument in *The Critique of Judgment* that the beautiful is the symbol of the morally good may be the most often and most profoundly misunderstood claim that this already grossly misunderstood thinker has written. That it might be true is possible only if the distinction between the good and the beautiful is already deeply established. What Kant definitely does *not* mean is that a beautiful story must present a moral message. The beautiful is the symbol of the good only because the moral is, for Kant, the purest and most direct access we have to *reason*; and insofar as Kant understands beauty as the harmony among the faculties, the rational, lurking in our perception as harmonious with it, pleases us simply as it is perceived, and not as it is applied or used in any way. Thus, we need not say that all morally good people are therefore beautiful, which would be inane, nor do we deny that many beautiful people are wicked; what we *may* say, however, is that the manifestation of courage, merely as a perceived event and not as an ethical quality, can be beautiful. This beauty in the external manifestation of courage becomes an essential part of our celebratory appreciation of fun as the coherence-rendering element in the comedic art. Since it is courage, however, it does enable nobility, especially in the young lovers, but also in the clowns.

It is now required, however, to examine critically the claim that fun establishes coherence in the unfolding of the comedic story; and to do this requires a grasp of the antithesis of comedy: nihilism. The prior suggestion that nihilism follows from the inefficacy of traditional ways of reasoning to give any authority to judgments about meaning must now be strengthened. After all, we are constantly discovering that reasoning has broader and richer modes than mere logic or science. We learn that wagering, idealizing, dialectical regression back to principles, and even inquiry itself are ways of reasoning, so that existence might be thought about simply because there are diverse ways of legitimate thinking. The philosophical nihilist is not content with arguing that reason is unable to handle existential questions; rather, he argues that reason itself does handle such questions and shows that there is nothing there. It is not that I cannot think coherence to my historical becoming—my temporal, finite existence that ends—but that there can be no coherence in the reality of my becoming. The refined nihilist may consider the previous argument about tragedy as valid, and exult: it is precisely because the access to meaning can be found only in art shows that it is not true. The storyteller does indeed add coherence to the temporal sequence of personal reality, which simply means it is not in the reality but in the telling. Art is a glorious, enjoyable, satisfying, egotistical deceit. The fact, the inescapable truth, is that we are mortal, and death, erasing me, erases my worth, my thinking, and what I falsely consider to be my contributions to anything worthwhile. The term "art" is contained in "artificial": it means: made up, fake, unreal, only pretense—hence, as fake it cannot be true. What is called fate or destiny or serendipity or luck or fortune or any other word borrowed from the ephemeral vocabulary of the elusive is nothing but coincidence; there simply is no coherence in the reality of such events at all. Granted we may give them coherence by painting them in the glowing colors of deceit—art—but such coherence cannot be *found* in them. To the suggestion that the theme of comedic art is graced folly, the nihilist shrugs, pointing out that the entire distinction between folly and wisdom is itself a sham; that grace may pardon our foolish errors assumes that what we call morality matters, which it does not. Stories come from storytellers, not from reality—and that sinks the ship.

But does it? There are true stories. Caesar really did threaten the republic, and Brutus and Cassius did kill him in the Forum. This act had consequences beyond Caesar's life. To say that Shakespeare's drama reveals how we can think about those real events does not mean that what enables us to think about the events is untrue while only the events themselves are true, any more than to say that the calculus that allows us to think about noncircular curves is untrue, and only the curves themselves are true. The error of nihilism is based, in part, on confusing actualism with realism, and nowhere is this made more obvious than in comedy.

Comedy is a story. Whether the events in the story actually happened or did not is irrelevant, since comedies as well as tragedies can be about historical, actual events or fictive, made-up plots. The difference, as noted above, is not between the fictive and nonfictive, but between the well-told and poorly told story. What is real, *and hence, when articulated, true*, is that we are fools, that we bestow and receive grace, and that we take delight in celebrating and hence sharing these truths. The nihilist need deny only the italicized words of this last sentence, but they are the ones that matter. In order for something to be thinkable it must be coherent; the telling of a story makes available, though does not make *up*, through articulation, a coherence or thinkability that is peculiarly well suited for unifying precisely those aspects of our existence that are not causally determined nor the result of purposive calculation. When this coherence, as a species of rationality, unifies precisely those existential aspects of our temporal becoming that seem to thwart the more practical uses of reason, especially those aspects we call folly and grace, the triumph is not of the irrational over the rational but of the rationality of persons over the rationality of events. This triumph, however, is possible only if the story is extremely well told, that is, told as a species of genius. We can call this comedic coherence wrought by the highest level of rationality, fun. It can be called fun because it ranks the coherence of persons above the coherence of events. We have already seen that one way in which we grasp the coherence of persons is in sharing: when Alan sees Mark dribbling the juice of his half of the shared orange on his chin they laugh in the felt joy of sharing, and this sharing is *fun*. To share is to belong together, it is to cohere as persons; its coherence provides thinkability.

If we say Mabel *is* fun rather than that she *has* fun, it suggests that fun is a way to be. The audience learns this way of being in the celebratory sharing of graced folly; for it is not merely that "things turn out happily" but that, in part, what enables the happiness is just the courageous embrace—hence graceful acceptance—of our own foolishness. The nihilist may look at the surface of the comedic plot and see evidence for his rejection of meaning, for his focus is on the unsuccess of human plotting. The Countess's and Sussanna's cunning to dress Cherubino as a girl to entrap the Count goes hideously awry; Rosalind's disguise as a young man puts her in a dreadful bind when she sees Orlando in the forest; Falstaff's lies put him in deep but hilarious trouble with Prince Hal. These scenes show how ineffective human planning is, leaving our existence entirely ungoverned and unthinkable—thereby supporting the nihilist's rejection of meaning. To rely solely on the success of human plotting is itself foolish, and if this reliance is the sole support of our assumption of existential thinkability, the nihilism inherent in this naiveté is fatal. What comedy shows us is that the very unsuccess of human plotting can be shared as a folly graced by the realization that we are more than what happens to us.

Causality is that species of rationality that provides coherence only to a sequential series of events; nobody denies that the bizarre events in a great comedy have causes; what can be denied is that such causal coherence is the only way we make things thinkable, and surely cannot be the fundamental way. Certainly it is not the kind of coherence that enables comedic truth.

In the opening chapter of this book it is noted that some theorists of laughter account for what is amusing by the apparent irrationality of human acts or even their combination with natural events. What we now realize is that laughter, at least in its comedic form, is not of irrationality but rationality on a higher level. This is a warm and joyous laughter just because it reveals our follies and our fondness as unified. There are various ways of unifying or cohering; but the supreme way is human sharing, so that sharing is existential coherence. The telling of a story, as artful, is thus not an invention but a discovery, a discovery enabled by seeing as coherent the emergence of our finitude as a folly that can be shared by being fun. To be fun is thus not a mere personality trait of certain bright and merry people like Mabel; rather, it is a way of being that enables sharing even by the normally stolid in the celebration of our universal truth as revealed by artists' genius. As a way of being that can be universally shared, it is, in the sharing, truthful. To suggest that fun is a way of being enables us to see it as the provider of coherence that is isomorphic to the tragic coherence provided by the sensed inevitability of fate. To suggest that fate in tragedy and fun in comedy provide the coherence as a result of art in no way entails that such coherence is therefore illusory or fictive, for stories are not merely the product of contrivance. This coherence renders the dramas thinkable, not merely in terms of their plot but also of character and theme: the art form brings all three together in a species of coherence that links its thinkability to its passionate responses. Reason here is no longer purely formal, and hence it is not set up against feeling, but is embodied in feeling. We do not sit in the audience and calculate in a purely formal way all these elements; they are felt as intense passions; but this passion does not divorce itself from the coherence that enables thought, but itself coheres with it. The dramatic synthesis of felt passion with authoritative reasoning is of such profound import that it deserves further reflection.

A live performance of *Hamlet* by thoughtful actors, unified by nonintrusive but faithful directing, usually succeeds in leaving the audience with a sense of dramatic coherence: the play works. Somehow or other, Hamlet's dark struggles with the enormous problems that beset all thinking mortals, seem to unfold in an enormously satisfying way. His death seems inevitable, though not determined; the play's final acts weave together many levels of human thought and feeling; as we leave the theatre we do not feel cheated: though the characters are remarkably complex and the issues deeply disturbing, as a d*rama* the last act finalizes; the ending makes sense, and the pathos of closure is inescapable. If someone in the audience protests a lack of emotional satisfaction the tendency is to blame the patron and not the artist. Yet, once away from the theatre, and removed by several days from the memory of the impact, the problems and irresolutions multiply like bees. Does Hamlet resolve the problem of divided loyalties, of man's peculiar destiny suspended between earth and heaven? Do we know exactly whether Gertrude was an accessory? Was Hamlet morally justified? The questions are left unanswered, though not entirely unilluminated. What seemed at the performance to be wondrous tensions, now, in reflection, threaten to become mere inconsistencies. Was our satisfaction at play's end, then, a contrivance? Was the emotional impact of all those bodies on the stage, in almost comic abundance, a distraction from the analytic precision we expect from thoughtful discourse? Surely not even Shakespeare himself would be able to unify all these profound ruminations on human destiny that seem, when we examine the text, to lead us nowhere. We still don't know whether it is better to be or not to be, and if that *is* the question, where is Shakespeare's answer? Is the dramatic satisfaction at play's end an answer? Or is it merely an *emotionally* satisfying end, an end that entertains; perhaps it is entertaining just because it lets us off the philosophical hook: now that Hamlet is dead we don't have to think about his horrible predicament—what a relief! Death may not answer these burning questions, but it may bury them. In burying them are we not placing tragedy in opposition to philosophy? The emotional satisfaction at play's end thus seems to become a nihilistic submersion of all thought into the vast, swallowing sea of oblivion.

The title of the play is *Hamlet*; it is not *Hamlet's Philosophical Questions*. Yet what offends in the previous paragraph is not so much the misreading of what drama offers—though that is certainly a part of it—but the even greater misreading of who the philosopher is and what it means to think. Only persons think—in spite of the defenders of artificial intelligence who would have us believe computers think, or the advocates of animal rights who protest that cougars and chipmunks think—but philosophers, as thinkers, are persons. What it means to think, then, cannot be exhaustively described by mere epistemology. To consider the activity of thinking—or worse, its mere formal criteria—without also asking what it means to think is simply itself bad thinking, for it offends by over-narrow abstraction. The challenge therefore is not to show that the play *Hamlet* is philosophically significant—of course it is—but to show that philosophical thought is rich enough to realize the truth made available by our celebrating the performance of *Hamlet*. This play, as a dramatic story, provides coherence to our own being in unfolding time; that its tragic end satisfies emotionally does not render it less coherent but more coherent. What would it mean to try to make sense of death solely in biological terms, without including such things as fear, dread, courage, wonder, hope, and even a sense of inevitability? To say these topics are emotional problems and hence not a part of truth or reason or thinking is ridiculous. Furthermore, in this particular play, the aesthetically inevitable death is of a man who not only has a certain inclination to philosophical thinking—and why should such characters be eliminated from the list of possible tragic heros?—he is also a man on whom the dire questions are forced: he *must* think about them. But he thinks about them as a whole person, not merely as a mind, and being a person cannot be separated from the emotional impacts that, in an art form, are essential for his story to be told. If the actual performance of this play alone provides that coherence that unifies both Hamlet's reasons with Hamlet's passions in the unfolding of his story, then such coherence cannot ever be merely formal, but *as* coherence it must be rational, that is, it must enable thought. Thus, the dramatic coherence itself is passionately rational, and not merely passionate *and* rational.

This passionate reasoning or even reasonable passion, in the unfolding of a dramatic story is also necessary for comedy. The coherence of passion and reason in comedy can be spotted as fun, as we say Mabel is fun. What is it that enables this way of being, called fun, that provides coherence? Mabel is able to extricate herself from the mere folly, or indeed even silliness, of Victorian mores, and reflect on it. Fun, therefore, is always to some extent the result of reflection; but it is a special species of reflection. It contains a certain degree of fondness for one's own belonging in what is reflected upon, coupled with a certain toughness that is realistic. Yet it is also playful, in the sense that we take delight just in watching people we love act in foolish ways because of love. This tough and playful reflection, however, is not the result of removing ourselves from our belonging, but involving ourselves more deeply in it. Reflection is often seen as entailing extrication, as if one must cease breathing in order to reflect on breathing. This way of thinking stems from the proper concern for impartiality in judging between contenders: we do not want gang members sitting on the jury deliberating the crimes committed by their gang lord. This concern, however, is valid only for special cases regarding advocacy; when extended beyond this, the demand for extrication becomes both obscene and absurd, creating a variation of what might be called the anthropologist's fallacy, in which the cultural observer has profound reverence for piety in every culture but his own. Reflection on one's own belonging cannot entail extrication of that belonging, any more than one indifferent to poetry can judge good from bad poetry. In stepping back from Victorian mores Mabel does not cease being Victorian any more than Auden's comments on other people's poetry makes him a non-poet. What allows for Mabel to reflect on her own participation in Victorian mores is her tough but playful fondness for her own belonging, and the folly inherent in such mores, a folly in which she shares. This reflection, by its toughness and fondness, reveals existential coherence between being in a comedic environment and looking at the same comedic environment. It is therefore not chiefly the characters in the play, such as Mabel, who fondly and toughly judge themselves, it is we the audience, who, as members of the comedic celebration, are enabled to judge in this profound way. And here we come to the nub: what enables us to judge on this profound level is comedy itself. Unless we are able to participate in the comedic celebration we cannot, in any other way, reflect on our folly with fondness to the extent that it discloses fundamental truth. The rare, existential coherence of being comedic judges of our own comedic folly—which is being fun at its highest level—exists nowhere outside of art; yet this coherence enables a truth that is so fundamental to what and who we are as foolish and hence rational persons, that, in its absence we cannot be complete, much less think about being complete. Fun enables us to be complete.

This claim that comedic fun enables completeness is troubling. It seems either to say too much or too little. Surely it says too much if we mean that the participatory celebration of our folly puts an end to our questioning. There are countless dimensions of our existence other than fun that, if absent, would render us incomplete: I am incomplete if I have never loved, or suffered, or forgiven, or solved a puzzle or even if I have never enjoyed Chateau Margaux. Yet these obviously true remarks also threaten to render the completeness enabled by comedy to be too little: fun is merely one of many, hence its import dims. Yet, in spite of these critical observations, it does not seem entirely unapt to suggest there is a sense of meaningful completeness afforded by comedy. The audience does not think that the final act of the comedy is the final act of the dramatic characters' lives—Figaro will go on to grace Rossini's opera, Falstaff reoccurs in later plays, and we like to believe that after the nuptials all in Arden will live happily—at least for a while. In what sense, then, are we to understand the suggestion that comedy completes?

All dramas, including but not restricted to, comedy and tragedy, are species of storytelling; and Aristotle's suggestion that stories have a beginning, middle, and end, seems, in spite of some contemporary experiments, still to have some validity. Is it this simple? Both the lives of the audience as well as the dramatic characters go on, but this particular story has an end? In one sense this is true: the specific problems that keep Claudio from wedding Hero or Orlando from joining with Rosalind, are resolved, and this resolution puts an end to the story that has as its thematic structure the unfolding of this resolution. That the problem is due in part to human folly is wondrously capped by the realization that the solution is also due in part to folly, for we miss the whole point if only the problem were foolish and only the solution were wise. Yet this remark in itself does not satisfy; for the joy of comedy is not primarily that taken in solving problems, even the problems that constitute an impediment to love's success. It is not the solution that elates the comic audience, but the whole story. Therefore it cannot be merely that stories have ends that accounts for the sense of closure or completeness that comedic fun provides. All stories have endings, but only comedic dramas—and not merely comedic endings—seem to offer this rather special sense of completeness.

It should not be overlooked that what prompts the present reflection on completeness rises out of the existential coherence inherent in the tough fondness that enables us to judge our own folly even as we are yet still foolish ourselves—which we provisionally identify as comedic fun. It is true that, in order for a story to provide coherence it must, in some sense, have an ending; what must now be realized is that the ending that provides a sense of completeness is not the resolution of the plot, but rather the sense of completeness thought and felt by the audience when the curtain falls or the lights go out. This completeness has already been identified as that joyous recognition of our own self-reflective judging of our graced foolishness. In what way is this recognition a species of completion? The first answer is that the recognition is not of solutions to problems or even a series of amusing events, but of existence itself. There are tellable stories within the larger, as yet incomplete, tellable story of our lives; and in one sense this larger story can only be told by those who live beyond us. In another sense, however, the greater story is made available to us even before we have completed our story; and this access is provided by the self-reflective act of judging our own folly with tough fondness.

The second answer to how comedy provides completeness is of greater philosophical worth. Fun, we have suggested, in its comedic sense comes about by sharing fondly our ability to judge and to be that which is judged, in terms of our folly being graced by the very act of self-judging. When we leave an inspired performance of a great comedy there is a sense of awe and wonder, coupled with a warmth and magic that amazes us; we are amazed because what prompts these sentiments or passions is our own judging ourselves as foolish. This judging is not of this or that particular plot, but of our own existence as finite. Since the judgment is not about the events, or even the characters on the stage, but of ourselves, there is created a sense of completeness. This is not completeness in the sense of being over, but of being whole. Our revels now have ended; we are complete because we have come full circle, not in the repetitive sense of doing the same thing all over again, but circular in the sense of being both judge and judged; not that there is nothing new, but quite to the contrary, it is all new again. Truth is a renewal. Our revels now begin.

Epilogue

OUR revels now have ended, and so they begin again. If the circularity of comedy is reflective of our finitude, we may wonder if the very nature of reasoning itself is involved with this closure. Can reasoning *as* reasoning be fun? This would seem to suggest that there is something foolish in philosophical inquiry. The misological millions sigh in long-delayed contentment: at last! From their own ranks we finally hear what we've known all along: doing philosophy is dumb: What fools these thinkers be! The indictment is not entirely without warrant; but neither is it a surprise. From its earliest beginnings, recognizing the shared spirituality of philosophy with the other Dionysian gifts, tragedy and comedy, the Greeks did not shy away from the inference. Their realization however is not so vague and abstract—talking loosely about a common spirit can mean anything—it is rather profoundly concrete.

He is very young; almost a boy, really; but highly gifted. His passionate love for his art is contagious, as he bubbles over with it in irrepressible enthusiasm. The fame he has deservedly won gives him a certain arrogance that, were it not for his genius and youth, would be a flaw; it is certainly a fault. Yet this arrogance seems so intertwined with his deep love for the poetry he recites so well we do not mind, just as we do not mind the barbs of insult between friends. We endure it, or perhaps even favor it, because it seems a mere echo of his great enthusiasm without which he would not be who he is. At the same time this cockiness becomes a resource for no little amusement. The old man speaking to him does not mind at all; indeed, he finds the boy endearing. With a certain amount of amusement we watch the old sage being genuinely astonished at the boy's gifts; and when asked how he does it, the boy himself is comically astonished he does not know. Mozart didn't know either, nor did Shakespeare; so why should we expect Ion to know? There is a great deal of warm fun in this playful, yet profound, query of a gifted genius whom Socrates loves. Yet, when professors and scholars insist on black and white characters, the boy becomes a model of error and iniquity, the old man a paradigm of knowledge and goodness. Socrates, we are told, is showing us how smart he is and how dumb Ion is; and this makes all the scholars feel superior and disdainful—even of Socrates; indeed even of Plato, for if that is how to read the dialogue it really is not worth reading. Socrates' astonishment was mere irony, they say; he really was not impressed at all. Armed with irony as an explanation, we can deconstruct the greatest and make everything banal. When I read this dialogue, however, I recall how astonished I am with artistic talent among the young, and find myself in awe at what I could never accomplish—how does this kid draw so beautifully? And when I ask him, we both seem slightly amazed he really doesn't know himself, and we laugh together at this realization: it is a moment of sharing that makes both of us glad. He draws so much better than I do, but he cannot question as well as I; but he *can* share in my questioning, for he hears in it a discovery of himself he had not known before, and I learn from his drawing a whole new way to see things; and this sharing is something only between us, establishing at least a camaraderie and possibly even the seed of a friendship; and that is just hugely precious; so I stop my ears if some pedant tries to defile it by asking who is superior to whom or suggesting its impropriety on the basis of the roles we play. Plato's dialogue, *Ion*, is comedic; it is also fun, and only as fun does it yield its remarkably deep secrets. For it is only when we recognize that Socrates really is amazed that the deeply troubling problem of genius becomes thinkable, and the metaphor of the magnet and iron rings shows it is as much the iron itself as it is the magnet that enables the art to work . . . but this amazement is rendered coherent only by the comedic union of folly and grace.

It is not, however, the *Ion* that is central. It is mentioned, not analyzed, here because it is easier to show its grace. So Plato, himself a dramatist, could write a comic dialogue—is that the point? It is the first step, not of a point, but of a great argument about the nature of truth—or to be more precise, about the nature of reasoning that leads us to truth.

Imagine this scene. There are two brothers, displaying in a public place their skill at sophistry. A crowd surrounds them, most of whom are laughing. Among them is a wonderful, older man, who is rather dour and a bit pedantic, but as loyal and as upright as one could ever hope for; he does not laugh at all, though; to him such playing is dangerous. In another part of the crowd, his old friend sits with a boy, both listening to the logical games. At first, this second older man worries that the dazzle of the brothers' cleverness may lead the boy astray, so he softly explains to the boy what the logical errors are and why these men are doing what they are doing. The brothers, though, are relentless, and soon they are making wilder and wilder uses of reasoning—or perhaps we should call it pseudoreasoning. The old man, Socrates, tries valiantly to refine their arguments with distinctions, but eventually he gives up. The crowd continues to laugh, and soon even Socrates laughs with them. He abandons his attempt to protect the boy Cleinias, and simply revels in the game. At one point the brothers argue that since Ctesippus's Father is father, he is the father of dogs. The onlookers howl, and Socrates is absolutely delighted. Crito, however, the dour old man who was kept from nearing Socrates by the laughing crowd, is mightily displeased, and after the group breaks up (enjoy the pun), chides the philosopher for abetting what seems to be the grossest form of misology. We should not forget this dour man, Crito, is the same who tries to convince his old dear friend to escape from the Athenian prison and go in exile to continue philosophy—so we know theirs is a deep, abiding, loving friendship that has sustained them both over many years.

What is Crito worried about? Was not Socrates himself at the beginning of the dialogue worried, too? Cleinias is very young; he should perhaps be protected from these mockeries of human reason, so precious to philosophers. Because a man is a father and dogs have fathers, therefore this man is a dog—indeed! What an insult. But does anyone really believe it, even for a moment? If the crowd believes it, why are they laughing? But what are they laughing *at*? Are they laughing *at* reasoning, hence mocking it? For Socrates to join in with them seems to make him an accessory to misology; no wonder Crito chides him. Euthydemus and his brother are bad enough making a mockery of reason, but Socrates is revered as a lover of reasoning, so for *him* to abet the scandal seems almost a sacrilege. To add insult to mockery, when the two old friends walk away from the agora, Socrates knowingly dissembles, claiming the young Cleinias had said something rather profound—perhaps to show Crito that the boy had not really been damaged—but it had not been Cleinias but an older person who had said it. Crito chides again, more heatedly and a little hurt, saying no mere boy could have been that clever, and Socrates, with a twinkle in his eye, nods and says Crito is probably right: it had not been the boy, Cleinias, who said it; he must have forgotten. Is not Socrates mocking dear old Crito in a cruel, unfriendly fashion? He does mock Crito, but not cruelly; it is, rather, a gentle poke at his friend's dour pedantry. Crito is not entirely dense; once Socrates confesses it may not have been Cleinias who spoke so wisely, Crito backs off, and shyly admits that because he cares so very much about his duty to educate his children properly that he felt uneasy about letting Cleinias be misled into misology. Dear, dear old and noble Crito: even his dourness is well intentioned, and Socrates is moved to comfort him, though laughter is still readier for the philosopher and he does not regret having poked gentle fun at his old friend. At the end of the dialogue, *Euthydemus*, even Crito senses, belatedly but yet genuinely, that perhaps there was fun in both the brothers' silliness and surely there was fun in his friend's sly kidding him. This is a sweet realization; it tells us a great deal about their friendship. If we read the *Euthydemus* prior to reading the *Crito*, this latter dialogue becomes far more intelligible.

What, though, does this reading of the *Euthydemus* suggest? That Socrates has a sense of humor? Or are we to study the dialogue as a resource of what later is to be known as informal fallacies? Aristotle will later codify some of these errors, providing great advantage to critics of bad reasoning. Is the dialogue a mere dramatic adumbration of Aristotle's formally superior work? Or can we now suggest that reasoning *as reasoning* is comedic? What would this seeming outlandish suggestion even *mean*?

Let us put aside the dialogue for a moment. I engage in a serious philosophical discussion with my friend; during this interchange I provide an argument that seems valid; but my friend points out that as stated, the argument is inconsistent with a prior argument both of us had agreed was sound. I admit the validity of his critique, and withdraw the argument in its present form. The question that seems to intrude upon us now is this: was my argument irrational? Was my suggesting it an irrational act? Was I being irrational when I suggested it? Or do we say only valid and perhaps even only sound arguments are rational? If so, when pressed, this would mean that a philosophical discussion that contains anything other than sound arguments is itself irrational, for if a part of an argument is invalid the whole argument is suspect; indeed, as a whole it is unworthy; it cannot lead us to truth.

This may seem like Congress reacting to a social ill that besets the nation; their draconian laws almost always imperil more than they rectify. It may be we need a distinction; perhaps the participlean form "reasoning," since it can refer to an actual event, should allow for bad arguments to emerge so they can be countered, and restrict the noun "reason" to that which must always be sound. This would make reason the ultimate mentor and critic of reasoning. It sounds like a good suggestion: indeed, it even sounds *right*. Surely, reason is a formal, law-like faculty that is the guarantor of validity and perhaps even soundness. What about "reasons," in the plural? Are they not already-tested arguments that are accumulated in texts or memory that we can use to make our inquiries coherent? It is as if a finite number of labelled inferences are written on cards in a file, and we can reach in and pull these "reasons" out to prop up or justify a claim. How did they get there in the first place? They were, we say, the product of our reasoning. But this places reasoning above reasons since it is only through reasoning that we discover which of the arguments are *reasons*. Which then is more fundamental? Reasoning as an activity? Reason as a faculty? Reasons as approved and licensed appeals? Is it not possible, through reason*ing*, to discover new and hitherto unexpected reasons? If so, it is reasoning and not reasons or even reason as a faculty that is prior. But reasoning, as an activity, must allow for arguments to arise that are eventually shown to be wrong just by the process of reasoning itself.

Reasoning as a process, however, is something we *do*, and we can do it in several ways. We can set up classical formal arguments in a syllogistic way, seeking to prove something; we can establish certain algorithms that allow us to arrive at certain desired results; we can adopt a harsh and critical scepticism testing another's systematic account of the whole; we can analyze something by breaking it down into recognizable and testable parts; we can use an established procedure such as the scientific method to assimilate evidence to support a hypothesis; or, we can inquire philosophically. This last way of reasoning as an activity may well be paramount. Here the general synthesis or overall coherence is achieved by a discursive critique in which the actual development of its authority necessarily contains suggestions, provisional accounts, and criticisms that themselves unfold in a noncausal but sequential story. To appreciate inquiry, then, one must first go through the early stages in which the problematic itself is revealed as a confrontation, then early suggestions are entertained and either rejected or, more importantly, refined, until, as the story proceeds, a certain weight or persuasion is brought about by the power of the story-like development, and either a resolution is reached or a formally superior level of asking requires a newer but more promising reexamination of the inquiry itself. This is reasoning as philosophical inquiry: on rare occasions the result of such reasoning is the isolation of a hitherto unexpected principle as the key to the entire possibility of coherence itself. Such inquiry requires the suggestion of alternative and even contradictory possibilities to show that the development emerges out of the conflict. Since the inquiry itself is rational we cannot say the presence within the dialogic process of suggestions that eventually reveal themselves as untenable because of the greater, discursive coherence provided by the story is an indication of irrationality or even improper procedure; quite to the contrary, unless both the sound and the unsound are part of the unfolding story, there is no discursive coherence at all. The threat to such discursive coherence, then, is not the presence within the argument of mistakes, but an unwillingness to follow through the unfolding or revealing story-based synthesis; this unwillingness is here identified as misology: the hatred or mistrust of reasoning based on the fact that within the story of thinking are mistaken—once believed but now rejected—parts. We recall that both Socrates early on and Crito throughout the *Euthydemus* were concerned that the boy Cleinias would become a misologist by hearing reason mocked.

Yet it is not the comic dialogues that provide the best reflection on this dilemma; it is rather the tragic dialogue, *Phaedo*, that offers the definitive analysis. Antigone is a tragic figure just because she is torn between two conflicting but legitimate loyalties from which, given her character, she cannot escape, so that her tragic end is the result of the plot-based conditions of her state, and the noble strength of her character not to escape from her destiny. Socrates likewise is torn between two loyalties: philosophy and Athens; the nobility of his character does not allow him to extricate himself, either. In both cases, the cruelty of their situations does not eclipse their worth, so that in the telling of their stories the triumph of their worth over their unsuccess attracts us to the unfolding drama. In the dialogue, however, the greatest threat to this triumph is the dark, emerging suggestion that reasoning itself may be a foolish way to live. Since Socrates' entire adult life was dedicated to such inquiry, the possibility of misology is dire indeed. Is his whole life a mistake?

Simmias and Cebes, two of the interlocutors of the Phaedo, point out that the arguments for the soul's immortality seem to have produced an equal persuasion that the soul is mortal. Why, then, they both ask, should we give reasons, or inquire philosophically, at all? Along with Socrates, they fear the possibility of misology; but it is the nature of his argument that is so stunning. He makes a remarkable analogy, comparing misanthropy to misology. In the glib, smooth readings of so may scholars, this telling passage is often dismissed as an aside, when in fact it is the very core and essence not only of this dialogue but of the five dialogues that make up the ending and justification of the Socratic life. Analogies work by comparing a relation of what is known to the identical relation in what is unknown. What we know—that is, what we are familiar with in our everyday life—is misanthropy—the hatred of the species mankind, including ourselves. What we want to learn about is misology: the hatred of our own reasoning. To make the analogy work it is necessary first to analyze what is wrong with misanthropy. Socrates calls it the worst state into which one can fall, for it makes our own existence wretched in the extreme. His analysis of this wretchedness or vice is brilliant, for it begins not with an inclination to discover our essential nature among the wicked and base, but among the noble and upright. If, Socrates points out, I focus only on men in their success, I prepare the way for misanthropy, simply because no human person ever is the ideal, and when I am forced to confront people as they are, the ideal is mocked, and the more I focus on the ideal the farther I remove myself from the real, enabling the false judgment that man, as he is, is loathsome and entirely unlovable. Therefore, the proper way to assess man is not solely in his goodness, but in his being both good and bad. We must learn from man his true nature, which is to be able to be both good and bad; in this we learn to love man as he is, hence in his truth, rather than as he is not, that is, in his artificial, abstract ideality, hence in his deceit.

This may seem at first glance entirely non-Platonic. Does not Plato, if not Socrates, insist on ideality as the highest form of reasoning, depicting ideal states or perfect love, scorning anything less than perfection? To object in this way reveals a profound misunderstanding of Plato's dialectic. To rank the kinds of souls or governments in the *Republic* is not to exclude any; it is to include them all. That they are ranked is necessary to discover how to think; but only a naive optimist—which is the prototype of the misanthropist—would exclude any of them. To love man therefore does not endorse his wickedness, for we still rank the good over the bad; but neither does it eliminate or forget his flaws. We *must* love the species as constituting all men: good, bad, base, noble, ugly, beautiful. Common reflection seems to support this analysis. It is remarkable that the downtrodden, the sufferer, the tough, and the sinner, are all more sympathetic to the human plight, even as they insist on absolute standards of right and wrong; but the elite, protected, spoiled purists, the well-favored and the rich, the lucky, the moral relativist, tend to despair of the human enterprise altogether. It is, perhaps, a fairly common realization—the surprise perhaps is that we find Plato defending it. If this suggestion makes sense—that the hatred of man begins in assuming that only the good are men—we are now prepared to make the analogy.

The love of reasoning must include its successes and its failures. If we see this as an analogy to misanthropy, however, it cannot be taken in its weaker sense, in which we simply tolerate suggestions lest we overlook something; or that given human finitude we might make mistakes. Rather, we are forced to adopt the stronger reading: in order for reasoning to be reasoning it must subsume not only mistakes due to our flawed nature, but the embrace of finitude within reasoning itself. This embrace is not merely of our being prone to error; it is rather the necessity of errors; for the great evil of misanthropy is to imagine ourselves capable of perfection, which then leads not only to a hatred of our present state of imperfection, but also to our own reality: to imagine myself without flaw is to imagine myself fundamentally other than I am, so that whatever achieves perfection is simply not me. To imagine reasoning without flaw is not to imagine reasoning but divine, direct insight. What I can do, however, is to embrace learning, and perhaps even refining and improving myself; and in this realization, I then can love myself with a fondness that includes loving the humanity as flawed within me. To love reasoning is thus by analogy—noting that analogy itself is a species of reasoning—to love the searching and inquiring after, and not the total possession of truth. This embrace of our flaws is akin to the fondness for our folly that is the essence of comedic art.

Plato, unfortunately, follows this profound analogy to misanthropy with a rather glib remark, apparently to soothe the discomfort of Simmias and Cebes, that threatens to unravel the argument entirely. He adds, almost as an afterthought, that we should perhaps distinguish reason from the reasoner, suggesting the fault lies not in reason but in our use of it. Three dangers lurk in this remark: first, that reason can somehow be thought as independent of the reasoner; second, that the errors are due to nonrational faculties; and third, that reasoning cannot in principle even be wrong. If this reading of the remark stands, the entire analysis of the analogue between misology and misanthropy is sabotaged. The most serious problem is the first listed: what would it mean to suggest reason is entirely independent of the reasoner? Is it some eternal force such as gravity, or an external, nonhuman entity such as God, or is it a preternatural power such as destiny or fate? Worst would be to suggest that reason is simply a metaphysical connection between prepositions. Surely Socrates cannot mean that reason is a real entity outside of human consciousness to which our thinking vaguely corresponds. What is far more likely, and acceptable, is the suggestion that as individual thinkers our own reasoning in a specific case may fail to achieve the standards of rationality that are available to our own thinking when more carefully refined. This solution also answers the second and third danger, and indeed can now be made compatible with the analogy between misanthropy and misology; in any event the analogy is far more important and profound than the caveat.

There is, however, a further point Socrates makes. Not only is there an analogy between misology and misanthropy; there is also a direct connection in terms of class inclusion: misology is a species of misanthropy. To hate my ability to reason is to hate my own humanity and hence to hate myself. This may seem a rather obvious point, but it is important to distinguish it from the argument by analogy. Further, it suggests an almost comic paradox. Simmias and Cebes are discussing the possibility of misology within an actual, ongoing rational inquiry. Are we, then, not involved in a circle? How can we assess the threat of misology without becoming misologists? In fact, this paradox is of remarkable profundity: the reader, as participant, is asked to adopt, however provisionally, the attitude of the misologist! Is this not highly dangerous, especially to a young, untrained reader? Are Socrates' moves sufficient to extricate us from the uncleanness of actually becoming misologists for a while? It is only when the reader directly confronts his own unease with an argument that supports both mortality and immortality that the extrication matters. We now realize why we must love man as both good and bad to avoid misanthropy, and love reasoning as a dialogic story honestly confronting the great problems greatly; only in this way do we achieve a true love of reasoning. We cannot truly dismiss misology until we have felt its lure, and perhaps even briefly yielded to its persuasion, for only by the experience of reasoning through the dangers is the triumph possible. In this sense reasoning should not only be able to thwart bad argument, it must be able to incorporate it in its unfolding.

It is now possible to return to the Euthydemus. The boy, Cleinias, learns there are fairly silly arguments which, even though they are wrong, have a seductive appeal. Resistance to this appeal is not that of the religious zealot condemning the sinner to hell, but of an astonished and amused lover of reasoning recognizing two indispensable characteristics of a philosophical inquiry: the mistakes are necessarily a part of being a thinker; the triumph is not over the mistakes only, but over an ominous nativeté that dangerously separates the thinker from his humanity. Only the comedic art form accomplishes this directly. The warm, self-mocking, delightful laughter that ultimately provides the ranking coherence of the dialogue can thus be seen as an essential part of its reasoning. Only thinkers as reasoners can laugh; only those who *do* laugh can think through an otherwise dangerous dialogue.

The minimalist may now admit that the two dialogues, *Ion* and *Euthydemus* succeed as comedic artworks; that is: only if we see them *as* comedic can we appreciate their reasoning. As a contribution to the historian this may suffice: we have learned something about these two works, and subsequently have broadened our appreciation of Plato's skill as a dramatic philosopher. Perhaps, however, such minimalist appreciation is too miserly: we might recognize that misology is a genuine and ongoing threat to all philosophical thinking, and that what we learn from the tragic dialogue *Phaedo* and the comic dialogues *Ion* and *Euthydemus* about understanding misology might be available only through such dramatic forms. Comedic dialogues, therefore, become essential for confronting misology, for only if it is possible to embrace first humanity itself with its folly and then reasoning itself with its developing through critical anti-reason, can we think through the darkness of misological dread and reach beyond it to the new dawn. This would be a far wider realization of the power provided by comedic art to the reflective thinker.

Perhaps, however, the learning is even deeper. It is possible to suggest that the very nature of philosophical inquiry per se, and hence not merely in cases concerning misology, must include comedic reflectivity. The need to reason at all marks us as finite: we must philosophically inquire only because we do not have direct access to complete and total knowledge, as God might have. This ignorance, necessary for inquiry, is a species of folly; to assume that reasoning can develop without confronting folly is precisely what leads to misology and hence misanthropy. What, then, is our attitude toward our own necessary ignorance? Inquiry itself seeks to rid us of ignorance, but it also reveals to us how we must think about what remains as ignorance. The pathos provided by comedy—and perhaps *only* by comedy—is the grace that enables folly to be embraced as part of our own nature. The philosopher therefore loves not only the truth, but also the truth seeker, who as seeker must be able to confront his own folly. In this sense, Socrates may be a greater advocate of true comedic genius than Aristophanes, for there is a warmth and fondness in the *Ion* and the *Euthydemus*, and perhaps the *Lysís*, and even maybe others, that is lacking in the more caustic and social buffoonery of *Lysistrata* and the *Clouds*. This suggestion does not entail the judgment that every dialogue or other species of doing philosophy must have comic elements; it does entail that our very understanding of ourselves as inquirers must somehow unify folly with grace.

A cautionary note must here be inserted. Graced folly is not a propadeutic to a softening of genuine moral censure any more than comedic dialogues abate the passion for truth. Awareness of folly is not a species of tolerance; or if it is, it is not the tolerance that abates our concern either with truth or with goodness. Just as true forgiveness is not possible without a vivid sense of the unacceptability of immoral behavior, so comedic folly enhances rather than mutes our concern for wisdom. When tolerance reaches the level of moral indifference it becomes intolerance, for letting cruelty thrive by lack of censure is the greatest intolerance of all; and letting ignorance thrive is not graced folly but graceless self-hatred. This is not merely a formal prop; it is part of our existential experience. Those who love comedy are not moral relativists or even moral weaklings. Folly itself cannot be tolerated at all; it can only be graced. We notice this in our everyday experience: those who would weaken moral censure are less, not more, likely to be moved by comedic genius. An audience that leaves a performance of *Le Nozze di Figaro* convinced that adultery is now acceptable is as puritanic as the pedant who would shut down the opera house for performing such scandalous fare. To realize that human reasoning must include suggestions that turn out to be untenable is to respect reasoning more than to assume that reason is simply a guarantee of correctness. Besides, even if reasoning that includes working through the untenable were not more respectful of thought, it is still the best we mortals have. It is our reasoning, human reasoning, glorified in the genius of thinkers such as Kant and Plato who do incorporate antinomies, untenable suggestions, and misological confrontations, that ultimately advances our learning to the highest degree. Perhaps we all dream for a Cartesian certainty, and find instead a self-reflective realization of rational struggle rather than rational success. Perhaps Mabel is forced to accept, not an ideal husband but a real, though flawed one, perhaps Cherubino never escapes his pain in loving or his exquisite doubts; perhaps Silvius will always dote on unworthy Phebe and hence never find the peace he seeks.

Perhaps my reflections are sound only for the very few comedies I discuss. I think they are universal because these few are paradigms and not examples; but even if they are only examples, so much is learned from them the effort is still worthy. It may be that most comedies do not grace human folly in a celebration of our own learning who we are; but these few, these precious few, certainly do. If this is so they should simply be performed more frequently and studied more assiduously. What we learn from these few, however, is of such universal import it is far less arrogant to suggest they are paradigms than that they alone, as mere samples, offer such wisdom. To suggest that the great wisdom learned from these few considered comedies is not universally available is elitist arrogance; insisting the wisdom is universal renders it available to all who think. To insist that only a minimalist, reductionist, comparativist account of comedies that applies equally to all comedies, even bad television sitcoms, is not more, but less philosophical. Only prodigious envy, the greatest enemy of the comedic, grumbles at the suggestion that some works are simply better than others. That we can accept favor in another without envy may be the finest jewel comedy offers.

In the final scene, Oberon bids his and Titania's fairies to bless Theseus's house:

> Now, until the break of day,
> Through this house each fairy stray,
> To the best bride-bed will we,
> Which by us shall blessed be;
> And the issue there create
> Even shall be fortunate.

We hear this without envy. When others are favored, and I am beset, two ways open: I can curse all unevenness, and wish for equality above all else, even if this sameness lowers all to my wretched state. Or, I can rejoice that some might be favored, even if it not be myself. The former's envy seeks the common as baseness in all understanding; the latter finds wisdom in excellence, seeking not the common but the universal. To see another favored without envy is grace; and it is a grace enabled by comedy. The house of Theseus is not the only place blessed—it is, after all, a fictive dwelling. The true blessing is on us, the true, dwelling audience. Thank you, Oberon.

INDEX

F

G

H

W

Y